Eco-economics II

Investing in a Youthful
Sustainable Market

By
Sowmy VJ

Foreword

Thanks for taking the time to read this book. I am Sowmy VJ, an asset manager based in London. This book is the result of extensive research since 2018, when I started noticing some key behavioural trends among the younger generation. I'd say my cutoff is at 30 years of age, but really as they started getting into the mid-30s as of now, they carried these behaviours with them. Their aspirations are clearly not met by the market, big brands don't recognise them as a unique customer segment, and they are often willing to pay more to fulfil their aspirations. All the way from where they live or aspire to live, what they choose to eat, how they commute or travel, and the products they use, it's a different world out there, from what they would expect. They learnt to be digitally native, using Instagram and TikTok, but work is nowhere close to that. As a result, their corporate employers can't expect them to have a long tenure. They start side hustles based on their interest and some of them are very successful at that. They are the Uber and Airbnb generation, yet real life means renting or mortgage, or long contracts. They learnt recycling, and sustainability at school, yet their flat is heated by gas, or the aircon is generating emissions. Most of the food on offer isn't sustainable. One of my research targets asked me why coffee is £3.50 and only goes down by £0.25 if you bring your own cup? Shouldn't it be £1.00 if you have a reusable mug?

Is there an alternative? Yes, there are products and services that cater to the younger generation. But they are few and super pricey in most cases. What can be done? We need to invest in tomorrow's economy. I wouldn't tell our son, Rohit to get a diesel car, just because it is the option available today. I wouldn't want him to take up a job with a large corporate who pollutes the world, throws a few peanuts to charity and gives two hoots to sustainability. Young people are hyper connected, global and willing to take risks, to ensure a sustainable future. If you have a child, would you invest in tomorrow's economy, today?

Dedicated to my best friend, soulmate, wife, co-founder, and ever supportive, Nithya Sowmy, and targeted towards those who want to invest in the aspirations of the younger generation, of which my son, Rohit Sowmy is a key participant. If you'd like to chat with me, please reach out on LinkedIn.

Table of Contents

Introduction

The global economy is undergoing a profound transformation driven by the energy, aspirations, and unique mindsets of the younger generation. As investors, we stand at the cusp of a new era where profitability and sustainability are not just compatible but symbiotic. This book aims to be your compass in navigating the complexities of investing in a youthful and sustainable economy, guiding you through the dynamic terrain where new opportunities are consistently emerging.

Today's youth are not just a demographic segment; they are the vanguard of change. They approach life, work, and consumption with a distinctly different set of values compared to previous generations. Their priorities lean heavily towards sustainability, digital innovation, and novel experiences over traditional product ownership. This monumental shift requires a fresh perspective on investment strategies that do more than just acknowledge these values—they need to harness them constructively.

In the chapters ahead, we will delve into various facets of this emerging landscape, starting with a deep dive into understanding the youthful global market. By grasping the economic and social forces shaping young consumers, investors can align their portfolios to not only mitigate risks but also leverage unparalleled growth opportunities. The future economy will be markedly different from the one we know today, with young people at its helm steering toward technology-driven sustainability.

1

Our journey begins with understanding the digital natives who wield significant influence over market trends. This generation's intimate relationship with technology renders them not just consumers but also creators of market disruptions. We will look at their preferences, behaviours, and the formidable impact they have on various sectors. The implications are vast and affect everything from retail and real estate to transportation and the food industry.

Next, we'll turn our focus to sustainability—a core value that resonates deeply with young people. They seek ethical investment opportunities that promise not only financial returns but also social and environmental dividends. This prevalent mindset is transforming how companies operate, compelling them to adopt eco-friendly practices and transparent business models. The book will help investors identify and capitalise on enterprises that align with these values, ensuring double-bottom-line benefits.

Experiential consumption is another trend gaining traction. The paradigm shift from ownership to experience signifies a move towards a sharing economy. Young consumers are less interested in owning products and more inclined towards accessing experiences that create lasting memories. This shift has far-reaching implications for investment, urging investors to reconsider ventures in industries such as travel, leisure, and entertainment, which offer lucrative returns.

Moreover, the interconnectedness brought by global connectivity is knitting different parts of the world closer together economically. The young generation, being global citizens, leverage this connectivity not just for social interaction but also for economic empowerment. They access opportunities beyond geographical constraints, spurring global economic growth. Understanding this dynamic can reveal strategic investments that tap into these interconnected markets.

Chapter after chapter, we will explore these influential factors in-depth, grounded in empirical data and enriched by case studies that exemplify successful strategies. For instance, we will look at disruptors like Octopus Energy, who are revolutionising their industries through innovative approaches that resonate with young, eco-conscious consumers.

The housing market for the young is evolving as well. We'll examine how this demographic prefers modular, flexible living spaces over traditional residential setups. Such preferences are reshaping real estate investments, dictating the terms for new kinds of housing developments attuned to their needs.

Transportation, too, is on the cusp of change. The younger generation's proclivity towards sustainability and efficiency is driving the surge in electric vehicles, ride-sharing platforms, and other innovative mobility solutions that present new opportunities for savvy investors.

The revolution in food consumption led by young people's awareness and preferences is spurring investments in plant-based and lab-grown alternatives. Companies that innovate in this space are now situated at the crest of a rising wave, poised for substantial growth.

Equally crucial is the role of education in nurturing this sustainability mindset. We'll highlight how educational trends are shaping business landscapes and what it means for future investment strategies.

Financial products, meanwhile, must evolve to meet emerging needs. Young investors seek products that are not only financially rewarding but also align with their ethical commitments. Offerings like green bonds, social impact funds, and cryptocurrency reflect this trend. Understanding these products and their implications will be pivotal in crafting future-proof investment portfolios.

The narrative woven through these pages will consistently circle back to one central point: youthful innovation and sustainability are not just trends but indelible features of the emerging economic landscape. The future is shaped by those who understand and adapt to these forces.

In essence, this book is not merely a guide; it is a call to action. It's a reminder that investing in a youthful and sustainable economy is not just about financial stewardship but also about contributing to a future that promises longevity, prosperity, and ecological balance. Our exploration will be rigorous yet inspiring, informative yet engaging, providing the tools needed to navigate this new economy with confidence and foresight.

As we delve into the following chapters, remember that each section builds on the preceding one to form a coherent strategy for future investments. Whether you are a seasoned investor or someone new to the game, the insights provided here aim to sharpen your focus, expand your horizons, and ultimately empower you to make informed decisions that will stand the test of time.

Chapter 1:
Understanding the Youthful Global Market

The global market landscape today is significantly different from what it was a few decades ago, primarily due to the emergence of a youthful demographic that commands both market influence and attention. Investors must delve deeply into understanding this demographic to make informed, strategic decisions. This chapter lays the groundwork for grasping the intricacies of the youthful global market, which is pivotal for driving sustainable investment outcomes.

Young people, often termed as "millennials" and "Gen Z," are reshaping economic norms through their unique consumption patterns, value systems, and engagement with technology. They are not only the most connected generation in history but also the most environmentally conscious. This generational shift is more than just a trend; it is a fundamental transformation in how economies operate, thus necessitating a different approach to investment.

One of the most pronounced characteristics of the youthful global market is their demand for transparency and ethical business practices. Unlike previous generations, young consumers place significant value on the environmental and social footprint of the products they purchase. They scrutinise brands and choose those that align with their personal values. For investors, this means that companies demonstrating genuine commitment to sustainability are more likely to succeed.

However, understanding the youthful market is not solely about recognising their ethical stances. It also involves appreciating their economic behaviours which often lean towards experience over ownership. Younger demographics prefer spending on experiences, such as travel, dining, and digital entertainment, more than on tangible goods. This shift necessitates a re-evaluation of investment portfolios to include sectors that cater to these preferences.

Another critical factor reshaping the youth market is technology. Digital natives navigate the digital landscape with ease, making them susceptible to rapid shifts in consumer behaviour driven by technological advancements. This dependency on technology for everyday activities – from shopping to socialising – signals a burgeoning market for tech-enabled services. Companies that innovate in these areas are likely to capture significant market share.

As we navigate further into this chapter, it is essential to highlight the geographical diversity within youthful markets. There is a tendency to generalise young consumers; however, regional variances play a substantial role in consumption patterns. For instance, while European youths may prioritise sustainability, those in emerging markets might focus more on affordability and access. For investors, this means adopting a nuanced approach, tailoring strategies that account for these differences.

Moreover, the economic resilience of the youthful global market cannot be overlooked. Despite facing challenges such as economic recessions and global pandemics, this demographic has demonstrated adaptability and resilience. They are quick to shift gears, embracing gig economies, and freelance opportunities which, in turn, redefine traditional employment sectors. An understanding of these developments can help investors predict market trends and adjust their strategies accordingly.

In discussing the youthful global market, it is also crucial to consider their role as employees. This generation is changing workplace dynamics by prioritising flexibility, work-life balance, and corporate social responsibility. Companies that acknowledge and adapt to these preferences not only attract talent but also foster loyalty and productivity. This shift directly impacts investor decisions related to human capital and organisational management.

Education and skill development also form a significant aspect of the youth market. Many young individuals are pursuing higher education and specialised skills training, often driven by the evolving demands of the job market. This trend opens up investment opportunities in education technology (EdTech) and skill development platforms, sectors poised for substantial growth.

Lastly, the youthful global market is characterised by a profound sense of global connectivity and cultural exchange. Social media platforms and digital communication channels have made it easier for young people to share ideas and influence each other's preferences globally. This interconnectedness means trends can emerge and spread rapidly, presenting both opportunities and risks for investors who must stay ahead of these global currents.

In conclusion, understanding the youthful global market is pivotal for shaping future investment strategies. Investors who pay attention to this demographic's values, behaviours, and aspirations will be better positioned to capitalise on emerging opportunities. The upcoming chapters will delve into further specifics of how digital natives are impacting investments, the sustainability mindset, and the significance of experience over ownership among younger consumers.

This foundational understanding serves as a springboard for exploring the multi-faceted dimensions of the youthful economy in subsequent sections. As we advance, the focus will be on actionable insights and strategies to navigate this dynamic and ever-evolving market efficiently.

Chapter 2:
Digital Natives and Their
Impact on Investment

The term "digital natives" conjures images of young individuals seamlessly navigating their way through a myriad of digital devices and platforms. Born into a world where the internet has always existed, these individuals—primarily millennials and Generation Z—display an aptitude for technology that surpasses previous generations. This chapter examines how this intrinsic familiarity with digital tools has redefined investment landscapes and what it means for future investment strategies.

Firstly, it's crucial to comprehend the sheer scale and influence of digital natives. According to recent data, millennials already constitute a significant segment of the workforce, and Generation Z is rapidly catching up. The purchasing power of these groups is on an upward trajectory, transforming them into pivotal players in global markets. Their economic influence is undeniable, which naturally extends to their investment habits and preferences.

Traditional investment vehicles—stocks, bonds, and real estate—still hold value, but digital natives are spearheading a shift towards more dynamic and varied financial products. Cryptocurrency, for example, has attracted significant interest from younger investors. Bitcoin, Ethereum, and a plethora of altcoins are not just speculative assets but a reflection of trust in decentralised systems. Unlike their predecessors, digital natives are more comfortable with the volatility and technological underpinnings of such assets.

Another noteworthy trend is the rise of fintech platforms. The days when investment required a call to a broker are long gone. Apps like Robinhood, eToro, Trading212, Moneybox, Nutmeg and Wealthsimple have democratized access to financial markets. These platforms offer a user-friendly interface, lower fees, and educational resources, making them particularly attractive to younger investors. The convenience and accessibility they offer cater perfectly to an audience that grew up with smartphones in hand.

Additionally, social media has dramatically altered how investment ideas are shared and proliferated. Platforms like Reddit and Twitter have given rise to communities where investment strategies and stock tips are discussed openly and in real-time. The GameStop short squeeze incident serves as a prime example of how collective action on these platforms can significantly impact market trends. For better or worse, digital natives are leveraging social networks to exert influence over financial markets.

Interestingly, digital natives are not just consumers but also content creators. Influencers and YouTubers are shaping investment narratives, offering reviews, and sharing personal investment journeys. This peer-driven content carries considerable weight, often more so than traditional financial advisors. Authenticity and relatability are key factors driving this trend, as digital natives are more likely to trust recommendations from someone relatable rather than a faceless entity.

Moreover, the ethical dimension of investing has come to the fore. Digital natives prioritize sustainability and social responsibility, and this values-based approach extends to their investment choices. Environmental, Social, and Governance (ESG) criteria play a prominent role in shaping portfolios. Companies that do not align with these values face the risk of exclusion. The message is clear: ethical considerations are no longer optional but rather integral to investment strategies targeting these groups.

In terms of specific sectors, technology remains a focal point. Beyond the obvious allure of big tech companies like Google, Apple, and Amazon, there's burgeoning interest in sectors like artificial intelligence, renewable energy, and biotechnology. These industries are perceived as not only lucrative but also as paving the way for future advancements. Digital natives want to be part of the next big thing, and these sectors offer them that opportunity.

Another emerging trend is the gamification of investment. Platforms like Acorns and Stash have introduced elements that make investing feel more like a game. By simplifying the investment process and introducing features like round-ups and micro-investing, these platforms have made it easier for younger individuals to start investing with modest sums. This approach demystifies the stock market, making it more accessible and engaging.

Despite their confidence in technology, digital natives are not immune to financial missteps. The combination of enthusiasm and relative inexperience can sometimes lead to impulsive decisions. Hence, educational initiatives remain paramount. Fortunately, a multitude of online courses and resources are available, helping to bridge the knowledge gap and promote informed decision-making.

Peer-to-peer lending and crowdfunding also reflect the communal aspect of how digital natives approach investment. Sites like Kickstarter and Indiegogo illustrate the power of collective financing. These platforms not only offer returns on investment but also contribute to projects in which investors genuinely believe. For digital natives, the emotional and social payoff is as crucial as the financial return.

Furthermore, we cannot overlook the impact of data analytics and AI in shaping investment strategies. Sophisticated algorithms can now analyse vast datasets, offering keen insights and predictions. Platforms utilizing these technologies provide users with tailored investment advice, aligning neatly with the personalised experiences that digital natives have come to expect.

It's evident that digital natives are redefining the investment landscape. Their comfort with technology, commitment to ethical investing, and preference for flexibility and community-driven platforms offer valuable insights for investors. Understanding these behaviours and integrating them into traditional investment models is essential for those looking to tap into this influential demographic.

As we've seen, the impact of digital natives on investment is profound and multifaceted. From fintech platforms to social media-driven market trends, their influence is reshaping conventional wisdom. Looking ahead, it will be vital for investors to align with the values and preferences of this generation, leveraging technology and ethical considerations to attract and retain their interest. Those who do so will find themselves well-positioned in an increasingly youthful and dynamic market landscape.

Chapter 3:
The Sustainability Mindset

The term 'sustainability' has permeated every corner of the modern financial landscape. This isn't just a passing trend but a new gospel for investors. The need for a sustainability mindset goes beyond environmental stewardship; it encompasses economic and social dimensions that are critical for the future. Investors who grasp this concept will not only align their portfolios with emerging market dynamics but also meet the ethical imperatives set forth by a younger, more conscientious generation.

Traditionally, investments were assessed on financial returns alone. Today, however, stakeholders expect a holistic approach, demanding that companies generate measurable social and environmental impacts. This paradigm shift is driven largely by younger investors, who are not content with compromising their ideals for short-term gains. They seek purpose, demanding that their investments reflect their values. For seasoned investors, this means adapting or risking obsolescence.

The sustainability mindset is not about making arbitrary sacrifices but recognising new opportunities. In a world where resources are finite and the climate crisis looms large, investing in sustainable solutions can offer robust returns. Renewable energy, sustainable agriculture, and green technologies are just the beginning. These sectors promise growth while mitigating the risk associated with depleting resources and stringent regulations.

Sustainable investing extends into social and governance factors as well. Companies that prioritise equitable labour practices, diversity, and transparency are increasingly viewed as stable and reliable. Investors should look at governance structures, ensuring that the companies they invest in are not just compliant but proactive in their ethical responsibilities. Neglecting this could lead to reputational damage and financial loss.

However, adopting a sustainability mindset isn't merely about negative screening, or avoiding 'sin stocks' such as tobacco and fossil fuels. It's also about positive impact investing. This involves channelling capital into companies, projects, or entities that are actively solving environmental and social problems. Such investments are not just mitigative but regenerative, laying the groundwork for systems that support long-term human and planetary health.

The metrics for assessing sustainability have matured, allowing for more precise evaluations. Environmental, Social, and Governance (ESG) criteria provide a comprehensive framework. Yet, while these metrics provide essential guidelines, they should never be used in isolation. Comprehensive due diligence remains paramount, as greenwashing—where companies dishonestly claim to be eco-friendly—remains a significant issue.

Another pivotal aspect of the sustainability mindset is understanding the temporal dimension. Sustainability isn't about immediate returns but about long-term value creation. This is crucial for younger demographics who are keen on future-proofing their investments. Investors must shift from a focus on short-term quarterly profits to long-term environmental and social returns. This approach aligns well with the increasing global focus on sustainability targets, such as the United Nations' Sustainable Development Goals (SDGs).

It's also essential to embrace the interconnectedness of global markets. Environmental and social issues do not respect national boundaries; thus, a global perspective is indispensable. Multinational corporations often operate within intricate supply chains that can obscure sustainability practices. Experienced investors must delve deep, scrutinising these layers to ensure that sustainability claims hold true from production to consumption.

Technological advancements also play a vital role in enabling a sustainability mindset. Blockchain, for instance, can offer unparalleled transparency in supply chain operations. Advanced analytics provide insights into potential risks and opportunities in sustainability investing. Investors should leverage these technologies to not only safeguard their portfolios but to engage actively in the transition towards a more sustainable world.

Moreover, the relationship between sustainability and profitability isn't mutually exclusive. Numerous studies suggest that companies with robust ESG practices tend to outperform their peers. They usually demonstrate better operational efficiencies, lower cost of capital, and enhanced employee satisfaction. Thus, a sustainability mindset should be viewed as a strategy to unlock new avenues of growth, rather than a risk minimisation tactic alone.

Changing consumer preferences also underscore the need for sustainable investments. Today's consumers prefer brands that reflect their values, driving demand for ethically produced goods. Investors should be attentive to sectors where this shift is most prominent, such as fashion, food, and tech. This alignment is not merely beneficial in terms of returns but is a moral imperative for shaping a more equitable future.

Furthermore, investors must consider the regulatory landscape, which is increasingly favouring sustainability. Governments around the world are implementing policies that encourage renewable energy, circular economies, and fair trade. Regulatory shifts create opportunities for early movers but can penalise those who remain complacent. Staying ahead of these curves isn't just wise; it's essential.

It's worth mentioning the risk management aspect of the sustainability mindset. Investing in sustainability doesn't eliminate risks but transforms them. Climate risks, for instance, though daunting, can be managed through diversification and strategic foresight. Sustainable investments can act as a hedge against risks that conventional investments are increasingly susceptible to, such as legislative changes and resource scarcity.

Lastly, fostering a sustainability mindset requires a transformative shift—not merely tweaking existing strategies but rethinking them from the ground up. This involves continuous education, engagement with emerging research, and fostering collaborations with stakeholders committed to sustainability. A mindset open to innovation and committed to ethical imperatives can unlock the true potential of sustainable investing.

In summary, adopting a sustainability mindset involves more than just reactive measures; it demands proactive engagement. For investors, this means reexamining traditional constructs and adapting to new paradigms. It's an embracing of long-term thinking, an appreciation for interconnectedness, and a commitment to ethical practices. Those who align with this mindset will not only witness profitable returns but will also contribute positively to the global economy, shaping a resilient and equitable future.

Chapter 4:
Experience Over Ownership

We've peeled back the layers of youthful markets, digital impacts, and sustainability. Now, let's delve into a seismic shift altering consumption: the rise of experience over ownership. This paradigm doesn't simply mark a change—it's a revolutionary upheaval with significant implications for astute investors.

Historically, possession equated status and wealth. Tangible assets—real estate, vehicles, luxury items—were coveted symbols. Today, this narrative is being rewritten. Younger generations are increasingly prioritising experiences. They're choosing to spend on travel, dining, and unique ventures over accumulating possessions. This isn't a transient trend; it's a generational redefinition of value.

What drives this shift? Several factors converge. Economic constraints play a role, as youth burdened with student debt and economic uncertainty opt for flexibility over long-term commitments. Yet, it's deeper than economics. Digitalisation and social media amplify experiences, fostering a culture that rewards shared memories over material gains.

Consider the meteoric rise of the experience economy. Platforms like Airbnb and Uber disrupted their respective markets by offering solutions that prioritise temporary, yet enriching, encounters. Airbnb forgoes traditional hotel ownership models, opting instead for providing unique lodging experiences shared by individuals. Uber's model isn't about car ownership but affording on-demand rides.

The investment landscape must pivot accordingly. Realising the potential of experience-centric businesses requires more than recognising demand shifts. It necessitates understanding how these businesses operate, scale, and retain consumer engagement. Unlike traditional sectors, experience-driven enterprises thrive on high customer satisfaction and retention rates, propelled by word-of-mouth and social media virality.

One notable sector affected is the leisure and travel industry. Youths are inclined towards adventure tourism, sustainable travel experiences, and culturally immersive activities. This drives investments towards niche travel companies, eco-friendly resorts, and tech platforms that facilitate personalised travel experiences.

Beyond travel, consider the implications for retail. Subscription models are reshaping how products are consumed, offering flexibility and novelty without the burden of ownership. Services such as Rent the Runway illustrate this pivot, allowing subscribers to access high-end fashion temporarily, alleviating the need for a large wardrobe.

Moreover, this shift compels an adaptation in marketing strategies. Experience-centric businesses leverage storytelling, user-generated content, and community-building tactics. Investment in such companies isn't solely based on financial metrics. It's about supporting platforms that master consumer engagement through emotional and experiential resonance.

Yet, this emphasis on experience over ownership doesn't imply the devaluation of tangible assets entirely. Rather, it signals a need for hybrid models. Real estate, for example, sees rising interests in co-living spaces, which blend the tangibility of property with the experiential richness of community living.

Investors must also consider technological advancements enabling this shift. Augmented reality (AR) and virtual reality (VR) offer expanded realms of experience. These technologies, once niche, now permeate gaming, retail, and education. Investing in AR/VR ventures or firms integrating these technologies positions one at the vanguard of experiential consumption.

Environmental implications also surface. Experience-driven consumption aligns with sustainable practices, reducing the volume of owned goods and, hence, waste. This intrinsic alignment can spur the growth of green initiatives and eco-conscious brands. Financing businesses that combine unique experiences with sustainability isn't just ethical; it's financially prudent.

Take, for instance, the burgeoning sectors of wellness and fitness. Beyond gyms, we see rapid growth in experiential wellness retreats, yoga workshops in exotic locations, and events such as marathons and triathlons. These ventures provide not just physical fitness but holistic well-being experiences, making them attractive investment opportunities.

The confluence of these factors requires a strategic approach to portfolio diversification. Traditional assets must coexist with investments in experiential ventures, creating a balanced but forward-looking portfolio. Dichotomous thinking—where tangible assets are inherently superior—must evolve.

Furthermore, understanding consumer psychology behind this shift is crucial. Anxiety and desire for immediate gratification drive the preference for experiences. In an age where social connections are increasingly mediated through digital platforms, shared experiences offer a form of authenticity and bonding that possessions fail to provide.

Segmentation within the youth demographic is also vital. Not all youth prioritise experiences uniformly. Tailoring investments towards specific sub-segments—such as urban professionals, digital nomads, or eco-conscious travellers—allows precision in capital allocation and maximises returns.

In conclusion, the legendary financier, Howard Marks, often speaks of the "second-level of thinking." Applying first-level thinking to this emergent trend would mean recognising a shift in consumer preference. Second-level thinking dives deeper; it anticipates how these shifts recalibrate entire ecosystems and where latent opportunities lie. It's a dance between appreciating ephemeral value and recognising sustained impact.

As we advance in this book, recognising the themes of connectivity, aspiration, and market adaptations will be critical. For now, embrace this knowledge: the age of experience over ownership is upon us. Investment strategies must not just accommodate but leverage this transformation. Only then will investors truly harness the vanguard of tomorrow's youthful and sustainable economy.

Chapter 5:
Global Connectivity and Its
Economic Implications

As we transition into a world increasingly interconnected by digital networks, the implications of global connectivity are reaching profound new depths. Investors who keenly observe these changes are better positioned to make strategic decisions that harness the inherent opportunities. The ever-expanding digital landscape is reshaping economies by erasing traditional barriers, creating a unified market that a savvy investor cannot afford to ignore.

The concept of global connectivity isn't just about widespread internet access; it's the seamless integration of economic activities, information flow, and communication across borders. This interconnectedness results in a more cohesive global economy, triggering shifts in consumer behaviour, production methods, and market dynamics. Businesses that once operated within local or national confines now have unrestricted access to international markets, enabling a more diverse range of products and services to reach a wider audience.

One pivotal aspect of global connectivity is the way it streamlines supply chains, cutting costs and improving efficiency. Companies can now source raw materials from one continent, manufacture products in another, and sell to consumers worldwide with unparalleled ease. This evolving model demands a keen understanding of logistics and supply chain management to ensure investments are optimised.

Consider how technology enhances traceability, from farm to table, or manufacturer to end-user, adding intrinsic value and reducing risk.

Moreover, digital platforms serve as the bedrock of this connectivity. Social media, e-commerce, and digital marketplaces are not just venues for communication or transactions; they are data-rich repositories offering insights into consumer preferences and behaviours. Investors attuned to these data streams can predict trends, tailor their strategies accordingly, and engage with markets in a more informed manner.

Another crucial driver is the proliferation of mobile technology. Mobile devices are becoming the primary interface for accessing the digital world, especially in emerging markets. These markets, significantly populated by a youthful demographic, are rapidly adopting mobile technology, leapfrogging traditional infrastructure. For an investor, this means new opportunities in sectors like mobile banking, fintech, and telemedicine.

However, global connectivity isn't without its complexities. With greater access comes heightened competition. Businesses must innovate continuously to maintain an edge. Intellectual property rights and cybersecurity become paramount, as do ethical considerations in data use and privacy. For the investor, these are risk factors to be meticulously evaluated.

The economic implications of global connectivity also extend to workforce dynamics. Remote work, facilitated by digital tools, has redefined the employer-employee relationship. Talent can be sourced globally, creating a competitive environment where skills and expertise transcend geographic boundaries. Investors might note which companies lead in remote work strategies, as these are likely to leverage a more diverse and resilient workforce.

Furthermore, global connectivity plays a critical role in fostering collaboration and innovation. Cross-border partnerships and multicultural teams fuel creativity and problem-solving, resulting in groundbreaking products and services. As an investor, identifying companies that leverage these collaborative advantages can provide a strategic edge.

In the realm of sustainability, global connectivity enables more efficient resource management and promotes eco-friendly business practices. Blockchain technology, for instance, can track the lifecycle of products, ensuring transparency and accountability in supply chains. Investors focused on sustainability can harness these technologies to back enterprises that align with their ethical standards and yield long-term returns.

Another major economic implication is the potential for financial inclusion. Digital platforms and fintech solutions are reaching unbanked populations, offering them access to financial services previously out of reach. Microloans, peer-to-peer lending, and mobile money are examples of how connectivity fosters economic empowerment. By investing in fintech innovations that prioritise inclusion, investors can tap into underserved markets and drive positive social impact.

Finally, the rapid evolution of global connectivity necessitates adaptive regulatory frameworks. Governments and international bodies must evolve policies to keep pace with technological advancements. As regulatory environments shift, investors must remain vigilant, understanding that policy changes can significantly impact market conditions. Engaging with thought leaders and policymakers can offer insights into forthcoming changes and how best to navigate them.

In summation, global connectivity is far more than the sum of its digital parts. It represents a fundamental shift in how economic activities are conducted and interconnected. For investors, the implications are vast. Understanding these dynamics—from supply chain innovations to the ethical use of data, from mobile technology adoption to the fostering of remote work and collaboration—provides a comprehensive framework for making informed, future-ready investment decisions.

This chapter has delineated the numerous facets of global connectivity and its far-reaching economic repercussions. The subsequent chapters will build upon these insights, delving deeper into specific sectors like transportation, real estate, and fintech, offering a granular look at how these overarching themes play out in different arenas. As you continue your journey through this book, keep in mind the foundational nature of global connectivity in driving the youthful and sustainable economy of tomorrow.

Chapter 6:
The Aspirations Gap

The disconnect between what today's youth aspire to achieve and what the market currently offers is growing. Investors must understand this chasm to bridge it effectively. Young people are informed and value-driven, seeking products and services that resonate with their ideals of sustainability and opportunity. Traditional investments often overlook this shift, offering outdated solutions that fail to engage a demographic hungry for meaningful innovation. Recognising and addressing the aspirations gap isn't just beneficial; it's essential for future-proofing portfolios. Investors must pivot to align with these evolving aspirations, embracing change and fostering opportunities that resonate with the values and ambitions of the next generation.

Bridging the Gap Between Youthful Aspirations and Market Offerings

The aspirations of young people today are remarkably transformative. Their desires are derived from a foundation of digital interconnectedness, a deep-seated demand for sustainability, and a penchant for experiences over material possessions. Yet, these very aspirations often clash with what's readily available in the marketplace. This dichotomy, referred to as "The Aspirations Gap," presents both a conundrum and an opportunity for investors.

To bridge this gap, it's essential to understand the nuances of youthful aspirations. Young people today seek authenticity and transparency. They value businesses that reflect their ethical stances and sustainable practices. Thus, the task for investors is twofold: identify companies that already align with these values and guide traditional firms to adapt to these emerging preferences.

One major area where youthful aspirations profoundly contrast with market offerings is sustainability. Youths advocate for eco-friendly practices and products, driving demand for sustainable brands and compelling the industry to evolve. This evolving market presents ample opportunities for investors to support green startups or incentivise established companies to adopt eco-friendly practices. Cash flows follow the green economy; hence, adhering to sustainability isn't just ethically sound but economically advantageous.

Sustainability is merely the tip of the iceberg. Young people are also highly digitised, creating a robust demand for tech-savvy, seamless experiences. From banking to shopping, the digital interface must be intuitive and efficient. Investors should seek ventures that innovate digital solutions and offer user-friendly experiences, underscoring the value of a well-integrated digital strategy.

While technology and sustainability dominate youthful aspirations, another critical dimension is the preference for experiences over ownership. Young people today are more inclined to spend on travel, dining, and activities rather than accumulating material goods. This shift predicates a growing market for experiential services. Investors should look at opportunities within experience-centric sectors such as travel tech, leisure, and wellness industries.

Bridging this gap necessitates not only understanding youthful aspirations but also reshaping market offerings to meet these needs. One approach is fostering collaboration between traditional companies and youth-driven start-ups. Such partnerships can help established firms integrate fresh, youthful perspectives and innovative solutions into their portfolio. On the flip side, start-ups gain scalability and market presence through these collaborations.

Moreover, market research and big data analytics play a crucial role in pinpointing youthful aspirations. By leveraging these tools, investors can glean insights into youth-driven trends and adjust their strategies accordingly. From predictive analytics to sentiment analysis, the capabilities of big data can assist in understanding and anticipating market shifts, thereby enabling more informed investment decisions.

A practical example of bridging this gap is seen in the rise of digital banking and fintech solutions. Traditional banks, often seen as cumbersome and outdated by young clients, are now evolving. Fintech start-ups offer streamlined services, from mobile banking to digital wallets, aligning perfectly with the digitally native generation's aspirations. Investing in such companies offers not only growth potential but also aligns with the youth's demand for technological innovation.

Yet innovation for the sake of innovation won't suffice. It's crucial to ensure that these innovations resonate with the underlying values of young consumers. Today's youth are discerning; they demand products and services that reflect their ethical and sustainable values. Thus, businesses that can demonstrate genuine commitment to these principles are positioned to capture their trust and, consequently, their spending power.

Taking a holistic approach also involves considering the broader, global context. The youthful demographic isn't confined to any single geographical region. Today's interconnected world means you're looking at a global market where trends transcend borders. Thus, an investment strategy focusing solely on localised markets might miss out on the broader picture. By understanding global trends and youth aspirations across different regions, investors can better position themselves to capitalise on emerging opportunities.

Furthermore, investment isn't just about financial gains but also social impact. Young people advocate for ethical investments and social responsibilities. They're more inclined towards brands and companies that contribute positively to society. Socially responsible investing (SRI) and environmental, social, and governance (ESG) criteria are critical lenses through which youthful investors view potential opportunities. Supporting businesses that adhere to these standards can help bridge that aspirations gap while realising substantial long-term returns.

The path to aligning with youthful aspirations and bridging the market gap isn't without its challenges. Resistance to change within established companies can stymie progress. However, those willing to adapt, innovate, and integrate youthful values into their business models will find that the payoff is worth the effort. Younger consumers are incredibly loyal to brands that align with their values, more so than any previous generation.

Investors also need to keep an eye on regulatory frameworks. Governments worldwide are increasingly implementing policies that encourage sustainable practices and ethical business operations. Staying ahead of these regulations can make a significant difference, as those who adapt early can benefit from incentives and avoid potential fines and sanctions.

Ultimately, the key to bridging the gap between youthful aspirations and market offerings lies in an investor's ability to anticipate and appreciate the broader socio-economic shifts driven by younger generations. This calls for a deft balance of pragmatism and visionary foresight. In doing so, investors not only curate a resilient and future-proof portfolio but also contribute positively to shaping a progressive and sustainable global economy.

It's about creating synergistic value—aligning market offerings to youthful expectations so that one complements the other. Whether through innovating new products, revamping existing services, or supporting transformative start-ups, the goal remains consistent: to build a market landscape that resonates with the upcoming generation's aspirations. This not only benefits investors but also establishes a more equitable and sustainable world.

To sum up, investors who adeptly bridge the gap between youthful aspirations and market offerings can expect to orchestrate a synergy that rewards both financially and ethically. It's a challenging endeavour but one fraught with unprecedented opportunities. The blueprint is clear: embrace sustainability, leverage technology, prioritise experiences, foster global insights, and ensure social impact. By doing so, you will not just keep pace with the market but lead it into a future shaped by the very consumers who define it.

Chapter 7:
The Free Market and
Consumer-Centric Models

The free market, often touted as the ultimate arena for entrepreneurial endeavours, places the consumer squarely at its centre. Unlike antiquated systems that prioritise producers, today's economy thrives on consumer feedback and evolving preferences. Investors must recognise this shift, understanding that capital flows towards enterprises that heed consumer needs and aspirations. This realignment offers a fertile ground for inventive business models that cater to today's conscientious and demanding consumer. By focusing on adaptation and responsiveness, investors can navigate the complexities of the market while fostering sustainable growth. As we delve deeper, the implications of this consumer-centric approach become ever more pertinent.

Why the Free Market Serves Consumers, Not Producers

The principles underpinning the free market revolve around voluntary transactions between buyers and sellers, driven by mutual self-interest. Many argue that the primary beneficiaries of this structure are the consumers, not the producers. As investors, understanding this dynamic is crucial.

In a free market, firms are compelled to innovate and improve continuously to cater to consumer preferences. This relentless pursuit of consumer satisfaction ensures that goods and services remain high in quality and competitively priced. Companies that fail to please their customers risk losing market share and, ultimately, their viability. Thus, the consumer holds a position of power, directing the flow of the market by rewarding the best-performing companies with their business.

Consider the technology sector, a vivid example of consumer-driven evolution. Companies like Apple and Google have thrived by anticipating and responding to consumer demands. By focusing on user-friendly interfaces, robust ecosystems, and cutting-edge innovations, these firms have secured their positions not by manipulating the market but by addressing the needs and desires of their patrons.

This consumer-centric model is not without its challenges for producers. Companies must stay ahead of trends, diversify their offerings, and remain agile in a rapidly changing landscape. The barriers to entry can be daunting, but it also ensures that complacency is penalised. While producers may occasionally wield significant market power, their success is ultimately tethered to their ability to meet and exceed consumer expectations.

From an investor's perspective, the focus should be on identifying firms that demonstrate a clear commitment to consumer satisfaction. These companies are more likely to sustain long-term growth and stability. Brands that captivate and retain a loyal consumer base often offer the most promising investment returns. Indeed, the stock market frequently reflects consumer sentiment, with share prices rising and falling in response to public perception and demand.

The sustainability movement provides another lens through which to view the consumer-producer dynamic in a free market. Increasingly, consumers are prioritising ethical standards, environmental responsibility, and social impact. Companies that align with these values are rewarded with consumer loyalty and financial success. Investors would do well to heed this shift, as it signals a significant redirection of market forces.

However, it is worth noting that the free market, in its purest form, doesn't inherently guarantee social equity or environmental sustainability. It operates on efficiency and profit maximisation, which can sometimes lead to negative externalities. Yet, as consumers become more informed and socially conscious, their purchasing decisions can guide markets towards more ethical practices.

Take the rise of organic and fair-trade products, for example. Once niche markets, these areas have grown substantially as consumers demanded more sustainably sourced goods. Producers had no choice but to adapt or risk obsolescence. This shift highlights how consumer preference can drive entire industries towards better practices, aligning business success with societal benefit.

In essence, the free market's emphasis on consumer needs leads to a more dynamic and responsive economic environment. The constant interplay between demand and supply fosters innovation and efficiency, with producers continuously refining their strategies to stay relevant. For investors, this consumer emphasis is a valuable barometer for assessing potential opportunities and risks within the market.

The automobile industry illustrates this consumer-centric approach effectively. Traditional car manufacturers like Ford and Toyota have had to reinvent themselves in the face of emerging electric vehicle (EV) companies like Tesla. The evolving consumer preference for greener, more efficient vehicles has driven a monumental shift within the industry. It is the consumer, not the producer, at the helm of this transformation.

This phenomenon is a testament to the overriding power of consumer choice in shaping industries. Even well-established market leaders must pivot and innovate when consumer preferences shift. Investors should recognise that long-term success often lies with companies that not only understand but also anticipate these shifts.

The free market also encourages a diverse range of products and services, catering to various consumer segments. This diversity ensures that even niche preferences can find fulfillment, further illustrating the market's consumer-centric nature. Producers that can identify and serve these niches effectively can carve out profitable positions, despite not being industry giants. For investors, spotting these niche opportunities can be particularly rewarding, as they often indicate untapped potential and growth.

In conclusion, the free market thrives on its ability to serve consumers. This foundational principle fosters a competitive, innovative environment where only the most consumer-responsive companies succeed. While producing can be a challenging endeavour, requiring constant adaptation and foresight, it is ultimately the demands and preferences of the consumer that shape the market. As investors seeking to navigate a youthful and sustainable economy, focusing on consumer-driven trends and preferences will be key to identifying resilient and prosperous investment opportunities.

Chapter 8:
Disruptors on the Horizon

In envisioning tomorrow's youthful and sustainable economy, it's imperative to recognise the disruptors on the horizon that will redefine industries and consumer behaviours. As these unconventional but powerful entities—like the innovative Octopus Energy—continue to emerge, they challenge traditional models and create new value propositions. Their transformative ideas are shaping a future where agility, sustainability, and customer-centric solutions thrive. As investors, understanding and identifying these disruptors can unlock unprecedented opportunities and drive resilient growth. It's about staying ahead of the curve and aligning investment strategies with the dynamism of the emerging market landscape. The forthcoming chapters will delve deeper into the specifics, but it's crucial to acknowledge that the disruptors we see today are the harbingers of the next economic paradigm.

Role of Disruptors Like Octopus Energy

As we navigate into new territories, the role of disruptors like Octopus Energy becomes ever so critical. These disruptors aren't merely unsettling traditional markets; they are creating entirely new paradigms of operation. Octopus Energy, founded in 2015, exemplifies how innovation and commitment to sustainability can merge to not only challenge but redefine existing structures in the energy sector.

Investors must take note: the landscapes these companies are creating are fertile grounds for growth, profitability, and sustainable impact. Octopus Energy leverages technology, data analytics, and renewable energy sources to provide competitive and transparent energy solutions. Their model profoundly contrasts with traditional energy suppliers bogged down by outdated infrastructures and operational inefficiencies.

The significance of Octopus Energy lies in its customer-centric approach, a hallmark of many modern disruptors. The traditional energy market operates on complex pricing structures, often to the detriment of consumers. Octopus Energy introduces simplicity and clarity, offering straightforward tariffs and no hidden fees. This transparency is particularly appealing to younger, tech-savvy consumers who demand ethical and straightforward dealings.

At the heart of Octopus Energy's disruptive approach is its investment in technology. The company utilises advanced algorithms to balance supply and demand, reducing waste and enhancing efficiency. Their agile software platform, Kraken, empowers rapid innovation, enabling them to quickly adapt to market needs and consumer expectations. For investors, this is where the value proposition intensifies. The agility and efficiency of Octopus Energy's tech infrastructure provide a competitive edge, ensuring they remain ahead of traditional counterparts.

Moreover, Octopus Energy's commitment to renewable energy doesn't just align with global sustainability goals; it aligns with consumer values, particularly those of younger generations. Profound shifts in consumer priorities towards sustainability and ethical consumption present significant opportunities for investors. By tapping into the ethos of companies like Octopus Energy, investors are not only securing financial returns but also contributing to a more sustainable future.

It's worth noting that Octopus Energy's disruptive potential extends globally. They've expanded their reach to several international markets, demonstrating the scalability of their model. This international expansion provides a diversified revenue stream, mitigating geographical risks and increasing overall market potential. Savvy investors will recognise the importance of such a diversified portfolio in managing risks and stabilising returns over time.

In addition, disruptors like Octopus Energy possess inherent adaptability. The energy sector has traditionally been sluggish, resistant to change, and bogged down by bureaucratic inertia. However, in today's rapidly evolving economic climate, adaptability is crucial. Octopus Energy's nimbleness allows it to navigate regulatory changes, market fluctuations, and technological advancements more effectively than traditional energy companies.

Investors should not overlook the consumer loyalty garnered by such companies. The personalised service, transparent pricing, and ethical stance resonate strongly with the youthful market. Customer loyalty translates into long-term revenue stability, reducing churn and marketing costs. These factors contribute to a robust business model that's attractive from an investment perspective.

The intersection of technological innovation and renewable energy is particularly compelling. Octopus Energy's use of data analytics to optimise energy consumption can be scaled across various sectors and applications. This potential for cross-sector innovation opens additional streams of investment opportunities. The energy market is just the beginning. The technology and methodologies pioneered by companies like Octopus Energy pave the way for innovations in transportation, real estate, and other high-energy consumption sectors.

Furthermore, the financial backing of Octopus Ventures, one of Europe's leading venture capital firms, provides an additional layer of security and confidence for potential investors. This relationship not only validates Octopus Energy's business model but also offers a network of resources and expertise, enhancing growth prospects. The collaborative dynamic between technology-driven initiatives and financial acumen makes a compelling case for investment.

One must also consider the broader implications of such disruption. As global energy needs evolve, the demand for sustainable and efficient solutions will only intensify. Octopus Energy's innovative strategies and commitment to renewable energy place them at the forefront of this transformation. Therefore, the potential for market share growth in an evolving energy landscape is immense.

Investors should also weigh the societal impact. The commitment to reducing carbon footprints and promoting renewable energy sources plays a crucial role in combatting climate change. Companies driven by such principles are likely to benefit from favourable regulatory environments, as governments increasingly support sustainable initiatives. Thus, the alignment with regulatory trends further enhances the investment potential in disruptors like Octopus Energy.

In conclusion, the role of disruptors like Octopus Energy extends far beyond mere market competition. They are reimagining what is possible in the energy sector by harnessing technology, prioritising sustainability, and meeting consumer demands head-on. For investors, this represents a golden opportunity to align financial growth with the tangible progress towards a more sustainable future. The continual evolution of the energy sector, driven by the innovative spirit of companies like Octopus Energy, is an avenue rife with potential, combining profitability with purpose.

Chapter 9:
Real Estate for a New Generation

The landscape of real estate is being redefined by a new generation of investors and inhabitants. These individuals prioritise flexibility, sustainability, and technology-driven solutions. No longer is property merely a static asset; contemporary buyers and renters seek dynamic living and working environments that seamlessly blend into their fluid lifestyles. The investor must understand these shifts to capitalise on emerging trends and meet the demands of this youthful demographic.

To begin with, environmental consciousness plays a critical role in property decisions. Today's young generation places immense value on sustainability. This group isn't just interested in eco-friendly slogans; they're looking for tangible green initiatives integrated into their living spaces. Properties boasting energy-efficient appliances, green roofs, and recycled construction materials are increasingly preferred. These features bolster property appeal and align well with governmental incentives and future-proofing strategies.

In our modern era, technology is a non-negotiable. Smart homes equipped with IoT devices, allowing for automated lighting, heating, and security systems, are more appealing than traditional properties. This tech-savvy generation considers connectivity a fundamental utility, just as crucial as water and electricity. Investment in real estate that prioritises robust digital infrastructure—from high-speed internet to cybersecurity—can yield significant returns.

Urbanisation trends continue to shift towards mixed-use developments. Younger generations value communities where they can live, work, and play without enduring long commutes or navigating sprawling urban landscapes. Properties that incorporate residential areas, co-working spaces, retail centres, and recreational facilities within close quarters attract this cohort. Such developments are not only convenient but also foster a sense of community, which is vital in today's fast-paced world.

Flexibility underpins modern real estate considerations. The popularity of short-term leases and co-living spaces is rising. Young professionals and digital nomads desire the ability to relocate quickly without being tethered by long-term commitments. Investments in flexible housing solutions—like fully furnished apartments available for short-term rental—cater to this demand, offering high occupancy rates and premium rental income.

Renting, rather than buying, is often the preferred choice for a substantial portion of this generation. Economic factors, lifestyle preferences, and the desire for mobility contribute to this trend. Investors should consider rental properties that appeal to young tenants—amenities such as communal areas, gyms, and social spaces add significant value. These features enhance tenant satisfaction and retention, ensuring steady rental income streams.

Co-working spaces represent another lucrative investment area. As remote work becomes more prevalent, the traditional office paradigm is evolving. Freelancers, start-up entrepreneurs, and young professionals favour flexible working environments that foster collaboration and innovation. Investing in or converting properties into co-working spaces can tap into this growing market, offering adaptable work environments that meet diverse needs.

Given the increasing importance of mental and physical well-being, properties designed with wellness in mind are particularly attractive. Buildings with ample natural light, green spaces, and wellness amenities such as yoga studios or meditation rooms are in high demand. Such environments enhance the quality of life, making them more appealing to young individuals focused on health and life balance.

Even location preferences are shifting. Traditional hot spots are giving way to up-and-coming, yet affordable, neighbourhoods. These areas often feature a mix of cultural diversity, artistic flair, and community-led initiatives, attracting younger generations seeking authentic, vibrant living experiences. Investors should monitor urban development plans and infrastructure projects to identify and capitalise on these emerging locations.

Let's not overlook the rise of alternative housing models. Tiny homes, modular structures, and container homes are becoming popular, driven by their affordability and minimal environmental impact. These options cater to the practical and ethical considerations of today's youth, making them worthwhile investment opportunities.

In sum, the real estate industry is undergoing substantial changes driven by the demands and values of a new generation. Flexibility, sustainability, technology, and community-centric designs are no longer optional; they're integral to modern property success. By heeding these trends, investors can align their portfolios with the evolving market, ensuring relevance and profitability in an increasingly competitive landscape.

Investors must stay abreast of these shifts to navigate the future real estate market successfully. Young individuals' needs and preferences, while varied, highlight a clear movement towards more sustainable, flexible, and community-focused living. Engaging with these trends will not only enhance property portfolios but also contribute positively to broader societal and environmental goals.

A strategic focus on these emerging trends offers not only financial returns but also the satisfaction of contributing to the development of living environments that genuinely enhance residents' lives. Our world is changing, and so are the places we call home. It's time for real estate investments to reflect this new reality, addressing the unique aspirations and challenges of the coming generations.

Chapter 10:
Revolutionising Transportation

As the dynamism of the global market intensifies, transportation stands on the brink of a profound transformation. For investors eager to tap into sustainable and futuristic economies, the transportation sector is both a fertile ground for investment and a linchpin of environmental recalibration. Our journey begins by exploring the catalysts driving this revolution and why strategic investments now could yield significant dividends.

Transportation isn't merely about moving people from point A to point B anymore. It encompasses a broader vision of improving efficiency, reducing carbon footprints, and transcending traditional modalities. Governments and private enterprises alike are funnelling immense resources into developing electric vehicles (EVs), high-speed trains, and autonomous driving technologies. These advancements are not just technological feats; they signal a paradigm shift in how we perceive mobility.

The shift towards electric vehicles represents a cornerstone of this transformation. Globally, the EV market is projected to grow exponentially. Governments are aggressively implementing policies that favour electric over internal combustion engines. Tax incentives, stricter emission regulations, and funding for R&D in battery technologies are catalysing this movement. From an investor's standpoint, companies involved in the production of EVs, their components, and the requisite infrastructure represent robust opportunities.

However, electric vehicles are only part of the story. High-speed rail networks are experiencing a renaissance as nations aim to offer faster, greener alternatives to air travel. In Europe and Asia, substantial investments in high-speed rail are reducing travel times and curbing the environmental impact of domestic flights. For instance, China's extensive high-speed network has not only revolutionised domestic travel but also serves as a blueprint for other nations.

Furthermore, the advent of autonomous driving promises to reshape urban environments profoundly. From increased safety to optimised traffic flows, autonomous vehicles (AVs) present far-reaching benefits. Tech giants and automotive companies are pouring billions into this evolving technology. Meanwhile, start-ups are emerging with innovative solutions for last-mile connectivity, which can significantly enhance the urban transit ecosystem.

For the keen investor, understanding the holistic market landscape is crucial. Electric and autonomous vehicles might dominate headlines, but the underlying infrastructure cannot be overlooked. Charging stations, smart grid enhancements, and data connectivity are integral components of this ecosystem. Investments in companies providing these ancillary services could offer stable returns and alignment with government grants and incentives.

Moreover, shared mobility solutions like ride-sharing and micro-mobility are reconfiguring urban transit dynamics. Companies such as Uber, Lyft, and various bike-sharing schemes have demonstrated the viability and commercial potential of the shared economy. These models not only aim for efficiency and affordability but also align closely with sustainability goals. As cities become increasingly congested, the demand for flexible and integrated mobility services will only grow.

One can't speak of transportation's future without acknowledging the critical role of data analytics. The abundance of data generated from smart vehicles, ride-sharing apps, and public transport systems is a goldmine. Advanced analytics and artificial intelligence can optimise routes, reduce travel times, and even predict maintenance needs. Investing in technologies that harness this data can yield significant competitive advantages.

While the opportunities are vast, investors must also navigate the inherent risks. Regulatory landscapes can shift, making once-lucrative investments less attractive. The volatility in raw material prices, especially those essential for battery manufacturing such as lithium and cobalt, presents another layer of complexity. Prudent investors will diversify, balancing high-reward opportunities with more stable investments in infrastructure and ancillary services.

In addition to environmental benefits, the transformative power of new transportation technologies can catalyse broader economic growth. Think of the urban expansions enabled by high-speed rail or the productivity gains from reduced commuter times via autonomous vehicles. These expansions create ancillary markets in real estate, retail, and local services, ostensibly multiplying investment opportunities.

From a global perspective, emerging markets represent fertile ground for innovative transportation solutions. Countries grappling with urban sprawl and congestion are ideal candidates for revolutionising transport infrastructure. Investments here can align not only with economic returns but also with broader developmental goals. For instance, India's ambitious public transport overhauls and Africa's rapid urbanisation present unique opportunities for forward-thinking investors.

Collaboration will undoubtedly drive the future of transportation. Partnerships between tech companies and traditional automakers, cross-border alliances for high-speed rail development, and public-private collaborations in setting up EV infrastructure will shape this sector. Investors who can navigate and leverage these collaborative efforts are poised to benefit the most.

In conclusion, revolutionising transportation is more than a trend; it's a seismic shift that defines the future of human mobility. The blend of technological advancements, policy incentives, and market demands is creating an environment ripe for investment. By adopting a strategic, informed approach, investors can not only achieve remarkable financial returns but also be part of a movement that redefines sustainability and efficiency in transportation.

Chapter 11:
The Future of Food

As we stand at the precipice of a new era, the future of food presents both a challenge and an opportunity for investors. The rapidly evolving landscape of agriculture, food production, and consumption patterns is influenced by technological advancements, sustainability concerns, and shifting consumer preferences. No longer can the food industry rely solely on traditional methodologies; it's imperative to embrace innovation to meet the demands of a younger, more conscientious generation.

One of the most significant trends affecting the future of food is the rise of plant-based diets. With an increasing awareness of the environmental impact of animal agriculture, more consumers are turning towards plant-based alternatives. Companies like Beyond Meat and Oatly have capitalised on this trend, offering products that appeal not only to vegans but also to flexitarians and omnivores. Investing in companies that specialise in plant-based foods isn't just a bet on a trend—it's a commitment to a sustainable future.

This shift towards sustainability extends beyond just what we eat. How our food is produced is undergoing a revolution. Vertical farming, for instance, promises to change urban agriculture. By growing crops in stacked layers within controlled environments, vertical farms use less water, require less land, and can produce food year-round, free from the constraints of traditional farming seasons.

Startups like AeroFarms and Plenty are pioneers in this space, and their success presents a robust case for investment.

Equally transformative is the field of synthetic biology, particularly the development of lab-grown meat. Companies such as Memphis Meats and Mosa Meat are leading the charge, creating meat that is biologically identical to conventional meat but without the ethical and environmental downsides of livestock farming. While still nascent, the lab-grown meat industry promises to be a significant player in the future food market, offering a potentially lower-risk investment with substantial long-term gains.

Technology is also playing a pivotal role in addressing food waste, a critical issue in the current food system. Approximately one-third of all food produced globally is wasted, a staggering statistic that represents both a moral failure and a missed economic opportunity. Innovations in food preservation, smart packaging, and supply chain management are all essential components in reducing waste. Companies developing these technologies, such as Apeel Sciences, which creates plant-derived coatings to extend the shelf life of produce, are not just solving a pressing problem; they are also crafting lucrative investment opportunities.

Another critical aspect for investors to consider is the future of personalised nutrition. The advent of data analytics, AI, and genomics has given rise to the concept of nutrition tailored to individual needs. Imagine a future where meals are designed specifically for your genetic makeup, lifestyle, and health goals. Companies like Nutrigenomix are exploring these frontiers, aiming to offer personalised dietary recommendations based on genetic profiling. The market for personalised nutrition is bound to grow, providing a unique niche for forward-thinking investors.

Sustainability in the future of food isn't limited to what we grow or how we grow it; it extends to our entire food ecosystem. Consider the role of packaging. Traditional plastic packaging is increasingly seen as untenable due to its environmental footprint. The development of biodegradable and compostable packaging materials represents a significant step toward reducing our reliance on plastic. This shift is supported by companies such as TIPA, which are developing fully compostable packaging solutions. Investing in these sustainable innovations is not merely ethical but also savvy, anticipating regulatory changes and consumer preferences.

Then there's the critical role of food security. Climate change, geopolitical instability, and economic disparity all pose significant threats to global food security. Technologies that enhance crop resilience, improve yield, and support sustainable farming practices are vital. Startups specialising in agri-tech, such as Indigo Agriculture, which uses microbial technology to improve plant health and productivity, are at the forefront of this movement. Supporting these companies aligns financial gain with the broader goal of global stability.

Furthermore, we must consider the importance of local and regional food systems. The COVID-19 pandemic has underscored the vulnerabilities of global supply chains, highlighting the need for more resilient local production systems. Community-supported agriculture (CSA), farmers markets, and local cooperatives are gaining traction, providing fresh, locally-sourced food with lower transportation emissions. Investments in infrastructure supporting local food systems can yield multifaceted returns—financial, environmental, and social.

It's essential to recognise the role of consumer habits in shaping the future food industry. The younger generation, particularly millennials and Gen Z, is more health-conscious and environmentally aware than previous generations. Their preference for organic, non-GMO, and sustainably sourced products is reshaping food production and marketing. Companies that align with these values will likely enjoy stronger consumer loyalty and market growth. Investors should look for brands and startups that prioritise transparency, sustainability, and ethical practices.

Moreover, digital platforms and e-commerce are transforming how we purchase and consume food. The rise of online grocery shopping, meal kit services, and food delivery apps have changed consumer expectations and behaviours. Companies at the intersection of technology and food, like Instacart and Blue Apron, are not merely riding a trend but are establishing new norms. Their innovative approaches offer significant investment potential, particularly as they continue to refine logistics, user experience, and service offerings.

Additionally, the concept of food as medicine is gaining traction. Leading health professionals increasingly recognise that diet plays a crucial role in preventing and managing chronic diseases. Functional foods—those offering health benefits beyond basic nutrition—are becoming more popular. Companies like BioGaia, known for its probiotic products, are pioneers in combining food and health, representing another promising investment domain.

In summary, the future of food is shaped by a myriad of interconnected trends and innovations. For investors, this sphere offers a diverse range of opportunities—from sustainable agriculture and advanced biotech to cutting-edge supply chain solutions and consumer-driven food services. The key is to recognise that the food industry is no longer insular; it intersects with technology, health, sustainability, and consumer behaviour in unprecedented ways. Navigating these intersections and investing in forward-thinking solutions not only promises considerable financial returns but also contributes to a more sustainable and equitable food system.

Next, we will delve into how these innovations and trends translate into broader industry adaptations, examining how existing corporations and new entrants alike are embracing sustainable practices to stay competitive in the changing market.

Chapter 12:
Industry Adaptations for a Sustainable Future

As we navigate the complexities of modern markets, the pivot towards sustainability isn't merely a trend—it's a necessity. Investors increasingly realise that traditional industries must adapt or risk obsolescence. It's a transformative period where economic viability aligns more closely with ecological responsibility. This chapter addresses the strategic shifts and innovative approaches industries are adopting to ensure a sustainable future, shaping tomorrow's economy.

In many ways, the concept of sustainability has fundamentally altered the investment landscape. No longer a peripheral concern, it now dictates core business strategies. Companies across various sectors are reconfiguring their value chains, placing an emphasis on reducing carbon footprints and promoting ethical sourcing. Investors must scrutinise these changes, assessing not only their impact on the bottom line but also the broader implications for long-term growth.

The energy sector is a prime example of adaptation in action. Once dominated by fossil fuels, it's now evolving to embrace renewable energy sources like solar and wind. Despite the initial capital intensity, these investments promise substantial returns over time. Additionally, they align with environmental targets set by international agreements, making them doubly attractive for forward-thinking investors. The rise of green bonds and sustainable funds further highlights how the financial world is underpinning these industry shifts.

Concomitantly, manufacturing is undergoing a seismic transformation. The adoption of circular economy principles signifies a move away from the traditional, linear model of 'take, make, waste.' Instead, materials are recycled, reducing waste and creating a more sustainable production cycle. This shift requires significant upfront investment in technology and process redesign, but it can result in reduced operational costs and less dependency on raw materials in the long run.

In transportation, adaptation is synonymous with innovation. Electric vehicles (EVs) are a central focus, but the sector's evolution extends further. Autonomous vehicles, shared mobility services, and advancements in public transportation infrastructure all contribute to a more sustainable future. For investors, these changes offer a mosaic of opportunities, from EV battery technology to smart city projects designed to enhance urban mobility while reducing emissions.

The fashion industry, notoriously one of the most polluting, is also responding to increasing pressures for sustainability. Brands are incorporating eco-friendly materials and adopting transparent supply chains. Beyond the operational changes, there is a growing emphasis on corporate responsibility. Investors can play a pivotal role by backing companies that not only innovate but commit to sustainable practices and improved labour conditions.

Retail, another significant sector, is reimagining its business model. The shift towards e-commerce, while not without its environmental challenges, opens new avenues for sustainability. Innovations such as zero-waste packaging, carbon-neutral shipping options, and the integration of blockchain for supply chain transparency are becoming more prevalent. These developments necessitate a critical eye from investors to identify credible commitments versus mere greenwashing.

Tech industry giants are not exempt from the sustainability mandate. Data centres, notorious for their energy consumption, are transitioning to renewable energy sources. Meanwhile, the emphasis on green computing is fostering advancements in energy-efficient hardware and software. Artificial Intelligence and Machine Learning are optimising resource use, leading to smarter, more sustainable business practices. Investors must navigate this domain with diligence, identifying tech innovators genuinely contributing to a sustainable future.

Financial institutions, pivotal in driving sustainability, have embraced Environment, Social, and Governance (ESG) criteria. ESG investing is no longer a niche market but a significant factor shaping investment decisions globally. From green bonds to impact investing, the financial sector is evolving to support and incentivise sustainable practices across industries. Such directions offer investors varied instruments to align their portfolios with sustainability goals.

Agriculture, ancient and modern simultaneously, is witnessing significant shifts towards sustainability. The emphasis on regenerative agriculture practices—those that restore soil health and biodiversity— marks a substantial deviation from conventional farming. Technological innovations such as precision farming and vertical farming are reducing resource use and enhancing yield efficiency. For investors, these practices not only promise better returns but also contribute to global food security.

Healthcare, too, is embracing sustainable practices. The advent of telemedicine reduces the need for travel, lowering carbon emissions. Sustainable pharmaceutical manufacturing processes and eco-friendly medical devices are under development. Furthermore, hospitals and health systems are investing in green buildings and operations. These advances present a dual opportunity for investors: promoting sustainability while ensuring the well-being of communities.

Consumer behaviour is a variable that industries continuously adapt to. As consumers become more eco-conscious, they drive changes in market demand. From the rise of the plant-based food market to the preference for sustainable packaging, consumer choices are pushing industries towards greener practices. Investors must be attuned to these shifts, as they often indicate the direction in which market leaders are heading.

The real estate industry is no stranger to adaptation. The adoption of green building certifications like LEED and BREEAM is increasingly prevalent. Such certifications not only ensure environmental compliance but also enhance property value. Energy-efficient buildings, smart homes, and sustainable urban planning are integral to the industry's future. Investors focusing on real estate must consider these factors to maximise their returns while contributing positively to the environment.

In the realm of finance, the adaptation has been significant as well. Impact investing and socially responsible investing (SRI) are gaining traction, offering investors avenues to support companies that align with their values. Financial products are increasingly designed to be transparent about their environmental and social impacts, allowing investors to make informed decisions. This shift indicates a broader recognition that sustainable business practices are not just ethical but also profitable.

Education plays a crucial role in facilitating industry adaptations. As more educational institutions include sustainability in their curricula, the workforce becomes better equipped to drive and manage sustainable practices within industries. Investors should view education as an essential pipeline for nurturing the talent required to support sustainable transformations.

While each industry's journey towards sustainability is unique, the underlying principle remains consistent: aligning economic activities with ecological imperatives benefits both businesses and societies. For investors, this alignment offers a pathway to robust, long-term returns.

As industries continue to adapt, the investment opportunities tied to sustainability will expand, presenting myriad possibilities for those ready to embrace a forward-thinking perspective.

Ultimately, the future of industry is bound to sustainability. It's not an optional attribute but an intrinsic quality that defines modern businesses. Investors stand at the intersection of influence and opportunity, with the power to drive meaningful change through their choices. The path may be complex and fraught with challenges, but the rewards—both financial and environmental—are substantial.

Chapter 13:
Financial Products for Emerging Needs

The landscape of financial products is rapidly evolving, driven by the unique demands of a younger, more dynamic market. Emerging needs require innovative solutions, and investors must keep pace to leverage these opportunities. Financial institutions, aware of the shifting tides, are crafting products that align with the values and aspirations of younger generations.

One of the most notable trends is the rise of sustainable investment options. Younger investors are increasingly prioritising social and environmental impact, and this is reflected in the growing popularity of ESG (Environmental, Social, and Governance) funds. These funds scrutinise companies not just for their financial performance but also for their commitment to sustainability and ethical practices. For investors, this means navigating through a landscape where financial returns must balance with moral returns.

Additionally, micro-investing platforms have emerged as a potent tool for democratising financial markets. Historically, investing was seen as a game for the wealthy, but the advent of platforms like Acorns and Robinhood has changed that narrative. These platforms enable individuals to invest small sums, making the process accessible to a broader demographic. By rounding up spare change from everyday purchases, users can accumulate investment capital that grows over time.

Decentralised finance, or DeFi, represents another frontier in this ever-transforming space. Built on blockchain technology, DeFi products eliminate the need for traditional financial intermediaries, offering services such as lending, borrowing, and trading directly to consumers. This model not only reduces transaction costs but also introduces a level of transparency and security that is appealing to digitally savvy, younger investors.

Moreover, the advent of robo-advisors has redefined the investment advisory landscape. These automated platforms use algorithms to offer personalised investment advice, which can be particularly appealing to those new to investing. The cost-effectiveness and efficiency of robo-advisors have made them a popular choice, enabling investors to maintain diversified portfolios without the need for traditional financial advisors.

Insurance products are also evolving to meet the specific needs of younger consumers. Usage-based insurance, for instance, tailors premiums based on real-time data, such as driving habits or health metrics. This customisation ensures that individuals only pay for what they need, making insurance more affordable and appealing to a cost-conscious generation.

Another burgeoning area is impact investing, which targets investments in companies, organisations, and funds with the intention of generating social and environmental impact alongside a financial return. This form of investing resonates with the values of younger generations, who increasingly seek to make a difference through their financial choices.

Peer-to-peer (P2P) lending platforms have introduced another layer of flexibility into the financial ecosystem. By directly connecting borrowers with lenders, these platforms bypass traditional banking institutions. P2P lending can offer more competitive interest rates and quicker access to funds, a feature that appeals to both sides of the transaction.

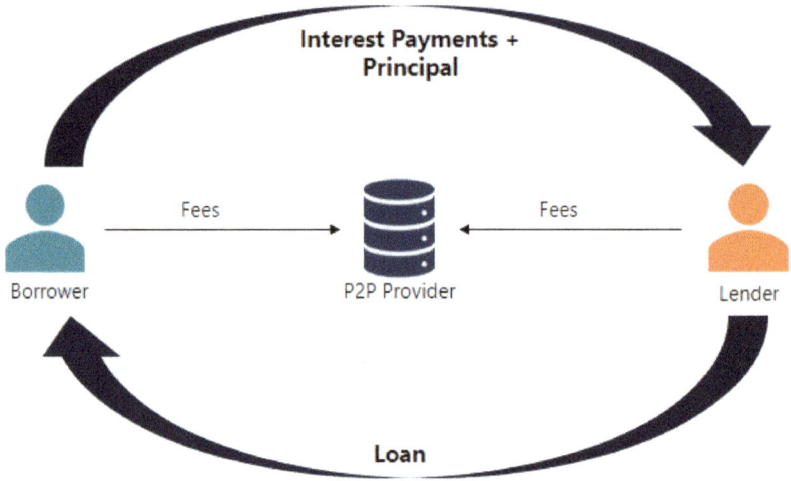

Furthermore, the incorporation of gamification elements in investment apps has garnered significant traction. By turning the investment process into a more engaging experience, these apps aim to educate users while making the often-intimidating world of finance more approachable. Features such as simulated trading environments, rewards for reaching investment milestones, and community challenges add a layer of interaction and fun to the process.

Cryptocurrencies and digital assets have also carved out a niche in the portfolios of younger investors. While volatile, these assets offer high risk-reward ratios and represent a cultural shift towards embracing new financial paradigms. Companies developing financial products around these assets are focusing on security and usability to attract this tech-savvy market.

Besides, subscription-based financial services are emerging as a novel way to offer products and advice. These services operate on a flat-fee model, granting access to a suite of financial planning tools and resources. This approach demystifies financial management, making it more comprehensible and less intimidating for young investors.

Still, the traditional banking sector is not being left behind. Banks are crafting tailored youth accounts and financial literacy programmes to captivate younger customers early. By offering tools and resources that educate on budgeting, saving, and investing, banks aim to build long-term relationships with this demographic.

Lastly, financial products focusing on health and wellness reflect the priorities of the emerging market. Wellness-linked savings accounts, for instance, reward individuals for maintaining healthy lifestyles by offering better interest rates. This integration of financial incentives with personal well-being has broad appeal.

In summary, the financial landscape is undergoing a significant transformation, driven by the emerging needs of a youthful demographic. From sustainable investing to fintech innovations and customised insurance products, the offerings are evolving to meet the values and aspirations of the next generation. Recognising and understanding these trends is key for investors looking to stay ahead of the curve in a rapidly changing market.

As we navigate this evolving financial ecosystem, the intersection of technology, ethics, and personalised services will continue to shape the products and opportunities available. Investors who embrace these changes and align their strategies with the emerging needs of the younger generation will be well-positioned to thrive in the dynamic market landscape.

Chapter 14:
The Impact of Education
on Sustainability

The evolving landscape of education directly shapes the ways in which future generations perceive sustainability. It is crucial to understand that education does more than just disseminate knowledge; it also cultivates attitudes and behaviours that are fundamental to the sustainable future we envision. The relationship between education and sustainability is symbiotic and complex, playing a pivotal role in fostering a culture that values long-term environmental and social well-being.

The integration of sustainability into educational curricula is gaining ground globally. Countries are increasingly embedding principles of sustainability into their education systems, from primary to tertiary levels. This trend not only nurtures environmental consciousness but also encourages innovative thinking and problem-solving skills aimed at tackling sustainability challenges. Educational institutions have become fertile grounds for germinating ideas that have the potential to revolutionise industries and markets.

Investors play a significant role in this transformation by funding and supporting educational initiatives geared towards sustainability. Such investments offer dual benefits: they not only contribute to the development of a skilled and conscientious workforce but also open up new market opportunities. By investing in educational technologies and sustainability programmes, investors are effectively seeding the next generation of eco-conscious consumers and entrepreneurs.

One notable aspect is the integration of experiential learning and hands-on projects. These educational approaches enable students to understand real-world implications of sustainability and nurtures a mindset geared towards innovative solutions. Projects that range from urban gardening to renewable energy installations provide practical experience which can be directly applied to entrepreneurial ventures or more responsible corporate practices.

Traditional business schools are also transforming, embedding sustainability into their core programmes. Business leaders of tomorrow are being trained not solely in maximising shareholder value but also in creating shared value that considers environmental and social outcomes. This shift transforms the investment landscape, driving demand for companies that are not only profitable but also purpose-driven.

Technology has emerged as a powerful enabler in making sustainability education accessible. Online platforms and digital resources have democratised access to knowledge, enabling a global audience to learn about sustainable practices. Edtech startups focused on sustainability are increasingly attracting investment, as they promise scalable solutions and broad impact. These platforms facilitate the dissemination of innovative ideas and best practices across borders, amplifying their reach and efficacy.

Of course, the impact of education on sustainability is influenced by cultural and economic contexts. Emerging markets, where traditional education systems may lack resources, face unique challenges in integrating sustainability into curricula. However, these challenges present investment opportunities. There is a burgeoning market for educational programmes and technologies tailored to these contexts, which can yield significant returns while driving meaningful social change.

Moreover, partnerships between the private sector and educational institutions can accelerate the uptake of sustainability education. Corporations that collaborate with universities on research and development projects can contribute to the advancement of sustainable technologies and practices. Such collaborations can yield innovative solutions that not only benefit the involved parties but also set industry benchmarks.

Additionally, lifelong learning and continuing education are becoming paramount in a rapidly evolving world. Professionals need to constantly update their skills to stay relevant, and sustainability is becoming a crucial part of this ongoing education. Investors can capitalise on this demand by supporting programmes that offer certifications in sustainability practices, renewable energy management, and corporate social responsibility.

Finally, we're witnessing a growing recognition of the role of early childhood education in shaping attitudes towards sustainability. Research supports the notion that attitudes formed in early years can have lasting impacts. As such, there are increasing investments in educational content and frameworks for younger children that prioritise environmental stewardship and social responsibility. Investing in educational toys, books, and media designed to instill these values can have long-term benefits, both societally and financially.

The impact of education on sustainability cannot be overstated. As investors, recognising and supporting this linkage unlocks a myriad of opportunities. From funding educational institutions and startups to investing in technologies that facilitate sustainability education, the prospects are vast and promising. In doing so, investors don't just secure profitable ventures but also contribute to nurturing a generation of informed, responsible, and innovative individuals dedicated to building a sustainable future.

In conclusion, the relationship between education and sustainability shapes not just individual futures, but the collective future of our planet. Strategic investments in this area pave the way for extensive and long-lasting impact, making it an indispensable focus for any forward-thinking investor.

Chapter 15:
Case Studies in Product Innovation

In the realm of investment, understanding product innovation yields invaluable insights. We don't just look at new gadgets; we examine how these products emerge despite often prohibitive policy environments. Take, for instance, a start-up that developed biodegradable packaging and bypassed regulatory constraints through agile strategies and adaptive design. Another example is a software company enhancing user privacy features, addressing both market demand and legislative frameworks. These case studies underline an essential truth: genuine innovation frequently transcends regulatory hurdles, providing investors with a roadmap for identifying resilient, forward-thinking ventures. By focusing on these real-world examples, we illuminate paths to investment success within an economy that's both youthful and sustainable.

Why Does Product Innovation Transcend Policy Obstacles?

In the ever-evolving landscape of global markets, product innovation often rises above the myriad policy obstacles that could ostensibly stifle it. This resilience is not merely fortuitous but a testament to the intrinsic qualities of innovation that attract investor interest. To comprehend this transcendence, one must recognise the underlying forces that drive innovation even in the face of regulatory challenges.

Firstly, innovation thrives on identifying and resolving pain points long before policy frameworks catch up. Innovators frequently lie ahead of the curve, visualising future needs and devising solutions that regulations have yet to consider. Policies are typically reactive, formed in response to existing conditions or problems, whereas innovation is proactive, creating new paradigms and thus staying ahead of legislative measures.

Take the case of the fintech industry. Traditions in banking and finance were upended by startups willing to challenge existing systems. These firms did not wait for favourable policies; instead, they exploited loopholes and unregulated spaces to introduce more efficient, consumer-friendly services. When regulators eventually stepped in, the innovative products had already garnered a significant customer base, oftentimes forcing regulatory bodies to adapt rather than inhibit such advances.

The adaptive nature of innovators also plays a key role. When faced with restrictive policies, product developers and companies can pivot, adjust, and sometimes entirely redirect their resources to navigate or even indirectly challenge these obstacles. Flexibility becomes a critical asset, enabling firms to not only comply with new regulations but also to find alternative methods to achieve their goals. This is particularly appealing to investors who value resilience and resourcefulness in their portfolio companies.

On the flip side, the economic inefficiencies generated by outdated or overly stringent policies frequently present opportunities for innovators. Traditional regulatory frameworks often bog down old industries, leaving gaps that new entrants can exploit. Consider the ride-sharing industry exemplified by companies like Uber and Lyft. Conventional taxi services were heavily regulated, and while those regulations were meant to ensure quality and safety, they also stifled competition and innovation. Ride-sharing apps skirted these regulations initially, offering better convenience and efficiency, which eventually led to policy adjustments rather than outright bans.

Furthermore, the global connectivity phenomenon contributes to the transcendence of product innovation over policy. With the power of the internet and digital communication, innovative ideas spread rapidly across borders. What starts as a local disruption can quickly become a global trend, compelling even the most rigid policies to reconsider their stance. Sometimes, the speed and scale at which innovation unfolds renders restrictive policies obsolete before they can even be enforced.

Investors should also consider the alignment of product innovation with broader societal needs and values. Innovations that address critical issues such as environmental sustainability, healthcare access, or social equity often receive public support despite regulatory challenges. This grassroots endorsement can push policymakers to revise or abolish obstructive regulations, as seen in the renewable energy sector. Companies like Tesla have faced countless regulatory hurdles but have successfully lobbied for more favourable policies by demonstrating broad societal benefits.

In examining case studies, it's evident that political climates and policy constructs differ widely from region to region. Yet innovation has a peculiar way of seeping through these variances. For example, China's stringent internet censorship did not prevent the rise of its tech giants, which tailored their innovations to comply with local regulations while still making significant advances. This adaptability showcases how innovation can navigate diverse policy environments, continually proving its mettle.

Regulatory obstacles also drive collaborations and partnerships that further strengthen innovation ecosystems. When single entities face resistance due to policies, forming alliances can provide the necessary leverage to influence change. Consider the pharmaceutical industry's recent strides in vaccine development amid the COVID-19 pandemic. Stringent regulatory requirements typically slow down drug approval processes. Yet through strategic partnerships, massive resource pooling, and an urgent societal need, innovative vaccines were developed and approved at unprecedented speeds.

It's equally important to recognise the role of cumulative knowledge and technological advancement. Innovations rarely occur in a vacuum; they build on previous successes and failures. This cumulative effect means that newer innovations are often more robust and better prepared to face regulatory scrutiny. The iterative nature of innovation ensures that each cycle produces more refined and policy-compliant products, thus gradually transcending policy impediments through sheer evolution.

Moreover, the benefits of innovation frequently outshine the constraints imposed by policies. Efficient market-disruption models often result in better consumer experiences, lower costs, and higher efficiencies, making it hard for even the most rigid policy structures to ignore. When an innovation demonstrably improves living standards, it places pressure on policymakers to adapt and allow such products to flourish. Investors are naturally drawn to ventures that hold this potential for substantial, tangible benefits.

In summation, while policies are essential for maintaining order and protecting public interests, their inherently reactive and slow-moving nature makes them less effective at stifling innovation. Product innovation, driven by foresight, adaptability, and public need, often transcends these barriers through proactive measures and strategic pivots. As an investor, understanding this dynamic not only clarifies the resilience of innovative ventures but also highlights the potential for significant returns even in highly regulated environments.

The empirical evidence is clear—product innovation doesn't merely coexist with policy obstacles; it often turns them into stepping stones. Adaptive strategies, societal alignment, and cumulative advancements make innovation a force that's incredibly hard to restrain, offering investors ample opportunities in an otherwise constrained landscape.

Chapter 16:
Policies and Their Economic Influence

Economic policies shape the investment landscape, acting as invisible forces that guide market behaviour and investor decisions. They are more than just regulations; they represent the intents and priorities of governments, shaping the broader economic narrative. Whether these policies aim to bolster sustainable initiatives or encourage business innovations, their ripple effects can't be overstated.

Strategic foresight into policy-making can provide investors with invaluable insights. These aren't merely regulations to comply with but opportunities to seize. A well-defined policy can promote growth in certain sectors while curtailing expansion in others, directly impacting an investor's portfolio decisions. Understanding these dynamics isn't optional—it's essential.

Take environmental policies, for example. Governments across the globe are now prioritising sustainable practices, driven by both public demand and climate imperatives. This shift provides fertile ground for investments in green technologies and renewable energy sources. Policies encouraging carbon neutrality not only make these sectors lucrative but also secure their long-term viability.

Monetary policies play a critical role too. Interest rates, inflation controls, and fiscal measures can all influence market conditions. Central banks adopting low-interest rates can stimulate borrowing and investments, resulting in more dynamic market activities. On the other hand, high-interest rates can tighten the flow of capital, leading to cautious investment behaviours. Investors need to keep a close eye on these signals to anticipate market movements effectively.

Furthermore, tax policies are a vital component of the economic framework. Tax incentives for specific sectors like technology or renewable energy can make these fields more attractive. Conversely, heavy taxation on industries seen as harmful, such as fossil fuels, can deter investments and shift capital to more sustainable sectors. These tax policies act as both carrots and sticks, guiding the flow of capital towards desired economic objectives.

Trade policies cannot be ignored. In an increasingly interconnected global economy, tariffs, trade agreements, and import-export regulations have profound impacts. Trade wars or restrictive policies can lead to market volatility, affecting everything from supply chains to consumer prices. Conversely, favourable trade agreements can open new markets and opportunities, fostering growth and expansion.

Labour policies also deserve attention. Minimum wage laws, labour rights, and workforce regulations influence the cost structures of businesses. Policies that prioritise fair wages and decent working conditions can lead to a more motivated and productive workforce, which in turn can impact the overall profitability and sustainability of investments. Conversely, overly stringent regulations can increase costs and reduce competitiveness.

Investors must also consider regulatory policies that govern market activities. Securities regulations, anti-trust laws, and disclosures add layers of complexity but also provide a safer investment environment. Transparent markets attract more investors and ensure a level playing field, crucial for sustainable economic growth.

Recently, data privacy and protection laws have emerged as significant factors. With the rapid growth of digital platforms and big data, regulations concerning data usage and privacy are transforming the economic landscape. Companies that can navigate these complexities and ensure compliance are likely to gain a competitive edge, making them attractive investments.

Equally important are innovation policies. Governments investing in research and development, fostering innovation hubs, and providing grants for cutting-edge technologies can create thriving ecosystems. These initiatives not only promote new businesses but also elevate entire sectors, creating vast opportunities for investors who are quick to recognise these trends.

Social welfare policies, too, have economic implications. Healthcare reforms, social security measures, and educational initiatives contribute to a more stable society, indirectly promoting a healthier economy. When people feel secure and supported, consumer confidence rises, leading to increased spending and investment.

In summary, understanding the multifaceted nature of policies and their ripple effects can significantly enhance investment strategies. Investors need to be astute in recognising these opportunities and challenges, aligning their portfolios to maximise returns while adhering to sustainable practices.

Policies aren't just regulations—they are the economic script guiding future market dynamics. They offer both challenges and opportunities, defining the playing field for wise investors. Keeping a keen eye on these signals can make the difference between missed opportunities and strategic success in tomorrow's economy.

Chapter 17:
Global Trends in Youth Employment

Consider the future of employment, and it's impossible to ignore the transformative effect of global trends on youth. The changes we're seeing today are unprecedented and unfolding at a pace that breeds both excitement and anxiety. Every investor keen on capturing opportunities in this youthful, ever-evolving market must understand these trends—not just to stay afloat but to thrive and lead.

Youth employment is intricately tied to the march of technology. Digital skills are at the forefront, with coding, data analysis, and digital marketing becoming indispensable. Young people are not only consuming technology; they are also shaping its evolution. With a smartphone in hand, today's youth are global citizens, unbound by geographic limitations. This shift necessitates a deeper dive into how technological advancements influence youth employment, especially in emerging markets where mobile connectivity outpaces basic infrastructure.

Understandably, traditional employment paradigms are rapidly losing relevance. The gig economy is on the rise, enabling flexible work arrangements that resonate with young job seekers. While this freedom is appealing, it lacks the stability older generations took for granted. Thus, one must weigh the pros and cons. Income can be unpredictable, but the adaptability of gig work fits seamlessly with the lifestyle many young people are drawn to.

For investors, the implications are profound. Companies facilitating gig economy opportunities—think Uber, Fiverr, and Upwork—are ascendant. Their growth signals a departure from conventional employment models, offering a fertile ground for investments that align with this workforce's aspirations. Yet, one must also consider the risk factors, such as the vulnerability of gig workers to regulatory changes and economic downturns.

Globalisation has brought its own set of challenges and opportunities. Youth in developed nations now contend with competition from their peers in developing countries. Jobs that once seemed secure have been outsourced to regions with lower labour costs. Simultaneously, this global connectivity has birthed massive collaborative opportunities. Teams scattered across different continents work together as though they were in the same room. As investors, recognising companies that master this global collaborative innovation is crucial.

Economic policies also have a significant bearing on youth employment. Countries that have embraced forward-thinking educational reforms are outperforming those stuck in archaic systems. Finland and Singapore come to mind, where education systems are designed to cultivate critical thinking, creativity, and technical prowess. These countries show how targeted investment in education yields a workforce that is both adaptable and innovative.

It's essential to examine how automation is reshaping employment landscapes. While this trend could displace certain jobs, it also creates new opportunities that were previously inconceivable. Automated systems handle repetitive tasks, allowing young employees to focus on roles that require creativity and emotional intelligence—traits machines cannot replicate. Companies at the forefront of harnessing automation, particularly those balancing tech and human elements, offer intriguing investment opportunities.

Social and environmental consciousness among youth cannot be overstated. The rise of the "green job" sector—comprising roles focused on sustainability, renewable energy, and environmental protection—is notable. Young people are not only seeking such jobs but also demanding that their employers adhere to ethical and sustainable practices. Investment in green technologies and companies with sustainable practices will likely yield significant returns, both financially and ethically.

In developing countries, the scenario is layered with complexity. Youth unemployment rates are often alarmingly high, presenting an array of socio-economic challenges. However, these regions also showcase some of the most innovative solutions born of necessity. For instance, social enterprises and organisations focused on skills training in Africa and South Asia are creating robust ecosystems that empower young people.

Investors should pay attention to these grassroots innovations, which frequently yield high returns and scalable solutions. For example, initiatives that offer micro-loans and vocational training can uplift entire communities, providing a new generation of skilled workers ready to engage with the global market.

Additionally, there is a rising trend of "youth entrepreneurship." Young people are increasingly disillusioned with traditional career paths and are instead opting to create their own businesses. These startups often disrupt existing market paradigms, presenting both opportunities and challenges. Investing in youth-led startups, especially in tech and sustainability sectors, can be lucrative. However, it necessitates a keen eye for genuine innovation versus fleeting trends.

Digital nomadism is more than a buzzword; it represents a fundamental shift in how the youth approach work-life balance. Armed with portable skills and a knack for technology, young people now traverse the globe while maintaining their careers. This trend has given rise to coworking spaces worldwide, presenting a niche yet profitable investment opportunity.

The rise in mental health awareness also shapes youth employment trends. Today's young workers value mental well-being as much as financial success. Companies offering robust mental health support and flexible working conditions are more attractive to this demographic. In turn, these companies often exhibit higher retention rates and increased productivity, making them appealing from an investment standpoint.

It is crucial to recognise that youth employment trends are interconnected with broader socio-political currents. The volatility of global markets, driven by everything from policy changes to economic cycles, significantly affects employment patterns. Young workers tend to be the first hit during economic downturns but are also highly adaptable and quick to seize new opportunities when the tide turns.

To summarise, investors keen on leveraging global trends in youth employment must adopt a multifaceted approach. Understand that the youth labour market is dynamic, influenced by technology, globalisation, policies, and socio-economic factors. Investments that align with these trends, particularly in tech-enabled platforms, green sectors, and youth-focused educational reforms, promise not just financial gains but also the opportunity to contribute positively to a sustainable and equitable global economy.

Ultimately, the aim should be not just to capitalise on these trends but to be part of the narrative that shapes a future where the aspirations of the younger generation are met with opportunities that lead to a collective, sustainable growth. The time to act is now, and the field is ripe for those ready to invest wisely.

Chapter 18:
Digital Economy and the
Young Investor

The digital economy is transforming the way we live, work, and invest, appealing particularly to the younger generation. For investors, these shifts present both opportunities and challenges. This chapter delves into how the digital economy impacts young investors and how they, in turn, are reshaping the landscape.

First, let's understand what we mean by 'digital economy'. At its core, it encompasses businesses and services that utilise digital technologies. This can include e-commerce platforms, digital payment solutions, gig economy gigs via apps, cloud computing services, and even newer realms like cryptocurrencies and blockchain. Market dynamics have shifted significantly, driven by innovation and the digital natives who are adept at leveraging these technologies.

Young investors, often referred to as millennials and Gen Z, bring a unique perspective to the table. They have grown up in the age of the internet and smartphones, and they expect seamless, intuitive interactions. This group is not just passive consumers of technology; they actively shape it, driving trends and demanding transparency, authenticity, and corporate accountability.

One of the critical ways the digital economy benefits young investors is through increased access and lowered barriers to entry. With digital platforms, investing has become more democratic. Start-ups offering fractional shares and zero-commission trades have sprouted, making it feasible for young investors to begin their investing journey with minimal capital.

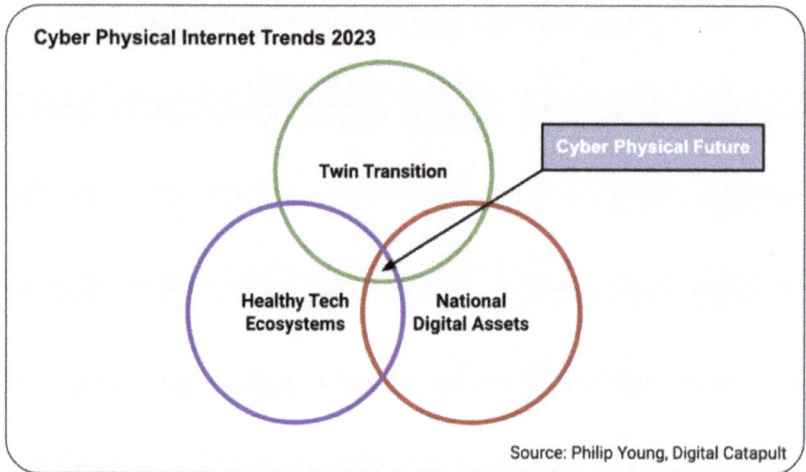

Cyber Physical Internet Trends 2023

Twin Transition

Cyber Physical Future

Healthy Tech
Ecosystems

National
Digital Assets

Source: Philip Young, Digital Catapult

This access, however, comes with its own set of challenges. The rapid pace of change in the digital economy means that what is cutting-edge today could become obsolete tomorrow. Young investors must stay informed and adaptable, constantly upgrading their knowledge and skills to keep pace with technological advancements.

Investing in the digital economy demands a keen understanding of various digital assets and sectors. Cryptocurrencies, for instance, have gained significant attention. While they offer high-reward potential, they come with equally high risks. Understanding the underlying blockchain technology is crucial for making informed decisions.

Additionally, the rise of fintech is another area where young investors must focus their attention. Companies in this sector are revolutionising everything from banking to insurance. The proliferation of robo-advisors is an example. These digital platforms provide algorithm-driven financial planning services with minimal human supervision. While they offer convenience and lower fees, investors should assess the algorithms' suitability and limitations.

Moreover, the digital economy has amplified the importance of data. Data is often referred to as the 'new oil', driving insights and decision-making processes. Young investors should appreciate the value of data-driven decision-making. Understanding trends, consumer behaviour, and market predictions through data analytics can provide significant competitive advantages.

Social media also plays a pivotal role. Platforms like Twitter, Reddit, and Instagram have become not just social hubs but also arenas where investing ideas are shared, debated, and sometimes hyped. The GameStop saga epitomises the power of collective action driven by online forums. While such movements can yield spectacular returns, they also possess inherent risks of market volatility and speculation.

Digital platforms have further revolutionised how we think about ownership and assets. The concept of tokenisation is a pioneering idea that allows for the digital representation of real-world assets. By breaking down assets into smaller, tradable units, tokenisation offers liquidity and accessibility, making it appealing to young investors.

Sustainability is yet another element intrinsically linked with the digital economy. Young investors are increasingly prioritising Environmental, Social, and Governance (ESG) criteria in their investment choices. The digital economy facilitates this by offering platforms that highlight ESG metrics, helping investors make informed, ethical choices.

Technology is also fostering innovation within the charity and social enterprise sectors. Crowdfunding platforms and blockchain-based charitable initiatives ensure transparency and accountability, resonating with the values of younger investors keen on making a social impact.

The workplace itself is undergoing transformative shifts thanks to the digital economy. Remote work, freelancing, and the gig economy offer flexible work models that many young investors are part of. This flexibility extends to how they manage their investments, opting for digital and mobile-first platforms that offer both ease of access and real-time updates.

However, this reliance on digital platforms isn't without its drawbacks. Cybersecurity threats are a pressing concern. Young investors must be vigilant about data privacy and safeguard their digital investments from fraudulent activities. Awareness and education about these risks are paramount.

The digital economy also brings forth an increased need for regulatory frameworks. While governments and regulatory bodies worldwide are beginning to catch up, there's still a degree of uncertainty, particularly concerning cryptocurrencies and digital assets. Investors must stay abreast of regulatory developments to navigate this evolving landscape prudently.

To thrive in this digital-driven investment arena, continual learning is essential. Online courses, webinars, and podcasts on digital finance and investing strategies are invaluable resources. Communities focused on investing can provide networking opportunities, mentorship, and support.

Ultimately, the digital economy levelled the playing field, rendering it possible for young investors to compete with seasoned professionals. Their natural affinity for technology offers them an edge, allowing them to harness digital tools effectively. However, this advantage must be balanced with an ethical, well-researched approach to investing.

As the digital economy evolves, so too does the profile of the young investor. Agile, informed, and values-driven, they are reshaping investment paradigms for a more connected, transparent, and inclusive financial future. Investors who recognise and adapt to these shifts stand to benefit from the boundless opportunities the digital economy offers.

Chapter 19:
Start-ups and Youthful
Entrepreneurship

In a world where technological advances are the norm and sustainability is paramount, start-ups driven by youthful entrepreneurship are no longer just a novelty; they are a necessity. The energy, ingenuity, and commitment these young entrepreneurs bring to the table can't be overstated. For investors looking to put their capital in ventures with long-term potential and societal impact, understanding the dynamics of start-ups led by young minds is crucial.

The entrepreneurial spirit has always been vibrant among the youth, but today's global connectivity and access to information have ignited it like never before. Young entrepreneurs, known as 'digital natives', are leveraging their familiarity with technology to create innovative solutions to contemporary problems. We see this across industries, from fintech and edtech to sustainable consumer goods. These young innovators are not just starting businesses; they are challenging the status quo and redefining markets.

One of the significant advantages young entrepreneurs have is their fresh perspective. They are not bogged down by the traditional ways of doing things, which often allows them to identify inefficiencies and opportunities where older generations might see insurmountable barriers. This open-mindedness makes them agile and receptive to new ideas, essential traits for the highly volatile start-up environment.

Furthermore, youthful entrepreneurs have an intrinsic understanding of the new-age consumer—largely because they are that consumer. They comprehend the demand for sustainability, desire for transparency, and necessity for social impact in a way that many established businesses struggle with. Their ventures are often deeply embedded with these principles from inception, making their business models more aligned with future market demands.

Beyond just identifying market gaps, today's young entrepreneurs are also well-versed in the art of storytelling. They can articulate their vision convincingly, often using personal narratives that resonate with both consumers and investors. This ability to build a compelling narrative around their brand and mission is a powerful tool in attracting investment and fostering consumer loyalty.

However, the journey of start-ups led by young founders isn't without its challenges. One of the most significant hurdles is access to funding. Traditional investors may be wary of placing their bets on unproven young talent, preferring instead to back experienced entrepreneurs. This is where forward-thinking investors can step in and make a discerning impact by recognising the potential in youthful ventures.

Investing in youth-driven start-ups requires a different approach. It's vital to focus not just on the idea but also on the team's ability to execute it. Investors should look for resilience, adaptability, and a clear understanding of market dynamics among the founding team. Diversifying investment portfolios with a mix of mature and youthful enterprises can also mitigate risks while embracing innovation.

Mentorship is another critical factor. Young entrepreneurs often benefit immensely from the guidance and experience of seasoned investors. This relationship should be symbiotic; while young founders gain practical insights and navigate early-stage challenges, investors stay abreast of emerging trends and fresh ideas that could shape the industry's future.

Collaborative ecosystems also play a critical role in fostering youthful entrepreneurship. Incubators, accelerators, and co-working spaces provide valuable resources and networks that can help young start-ups thrive. Investors should pay attention to these environments as they often serve as nurseries for the most promising ideas and innovations. By supporting such ecosystems, investors can indirectly influence the growth and success of numerous potential ventures.

Moreover, it's important to consider the global landscape. While Silicon Valley has long been the epicentre of start-up culture, innovation isn't confined to any single geography. Cities like Berlin, Bangalore, and Nairobi are emerging as hotbeds of entrepreneurial activity. Each of these ecosystems has its unique strengths and challenges that investors should understand to make informed decisions.

Another aspect to keep in mind is the focus on social entrepreneurship among young founders. They're not just keen on making profits; they want their ventures to have a positive social impact. Whether it's tackling climate change, improving healthcare access, or boosting education, these start-ups are inherently mission-driven. This convergence of profit and purpose presents a compelling proposition for investors interested in creating not just financial returns but also societal value.

Investors should also be aware of the regulatory landscape. While the youthful exuberance of these start-ups is a significant asset, it can sometimes lead to oversight of legal and regulatory requirements. Comprehensive due diligence and proactive engagement with regulatory bodies can help manage these risks effectively.

Lastly, the role of technology can't be understated. Today's start-ups are leveraging advancements in artificial intelligence, blockchain, and data analytics to drive their innovation. Understanding the technological underpinnings of these ventures can help investors assess their scalability and potential for disruption more accurately.

To summarise, start-ups and youthful entrepreneurship embody a powerful wave of innovation capable of reshaping our economy and society. By understanding and embracing the unique dynamics that these young entrepreneurs bring, investors can position themselves at the forefront of this transformative wave. It's not merely about funding the next big idea but about shaping the future by supporting those who are bold enough to create it.

Chapter 20:
Tech-Enabled Investment
Opportunities

As we advance deeper into the 21st century, technology's role in shaping investment landscapes has never been more profound. Today's investors need to grasp that we're standing on the precipice of a new era—a time when tech-enabled investment opportunities are driving a tidal wave of economic transformation. Capitalising on these changes requires not just understanding the technologies themselves, but also the underlying trends and societal transitions they foster.

From artificial intelligence to blockchain, the array of technological advancements offers a multitude of avenues for investment. One key area gaining traction is Artificial Intelligence (AI). AI represents a paradigm shift, promising to revolutionise industries by enhancing efficiency and innovation. For investors, this means an opportunity to support ventures that integrate AI, thus driving automation and analytics to unprecedented levels.

The application of AI isn't limited to high-tech firms alone; it stretches across diverse sectors, from healthcare to finance. For example, in healthcare, AI-powered diagnostic tools can improve accuracy and personalised treatment plans, ultimately leading to better patient outcomes. Investing in healthcare startups that leverage AI can thus generate substantial returns while contributing to societal good.

Blockchain technology, another cornerstone of modern innovation, is redefining how we think about trust and transparency. Best known as the backbone of cryptocurrencies, blockchain's decentralised nature offers secure and transparent transaction records. Beyond just digital currencies, blockchain is making significant inroads into supply chain management, providing a verifiable and immutable ledger that enhances accountability.

Investors should not overlook the potential of blockchain technology in transforming various industries. Enhanced traceability in supply chains, for example, can lead to more sustainable practices. By investing in blockchain solutions, one endorses a system that promises to reduce fraud, lower costs, and increase efficiency, marking a significant departure from traditional methods.

The Internet of Things (IoT) is yet another evolving sector ripe with opportunity. IoT refers to the interconnected world of devices, from home appliances to industrial machines, all communicating and exchanging data over the internet. This connectivity can lead to smarter cities and more efficient industrial operations, streamlining processes and cutting costs.

For instance, smart grids enabled by IoT can optimise energy consumption, balancing demand and supply more effectively, and hence reducing waste. Investors can support companies pioneering IoT solutions, particularly those focused on sustainability and efficiency. These ventures often reward with both economic returns and positive environmental impacts.

Moreover, sectors like fintech are experiencing a renaissance, thanks to technological integration. The rise of mobile payments, peer-to-peer lending platforms, and robo-advisors are making financial services more accessible and efficient. By leveraging data, these innovations are democratising finance, opening the doors to previously underserved markets.

Digital currencies are another aspect of fintech that deserves attention. Although volatile, cryptocurrencies present an intriguing investment opportunity. Their decentralised structure challenges traditional banking systems, and as more institutions explore blockchain for transactional security, the potential for growth is significant. However, this space requires cautious and informed investment decisions due to its inherent volatility and regulatory uncertainties.

Next, consider the role of 5G technology. The advent of 5G is not just about faster internet speeds; it's a crucial enabler for other technologies like AI, IoT, and autonomous vehicles. The seamless connectivity provided by 5G will drive innovation in ways we've yet to fully comprehend. As investment avenues, companies focused on rolling out 5G infrastructure or those developing products that leverage 5G capabilities hold significant promise.

Renewable energy technology also presents lucrative investment opportunities. Solar panels, wind turbines, and other green technologies are crucial in combating climate change. The advancements in energy storage solutions, such as improved battery technologies, are making renewable energy more viable and sustainable. Investors can explore these options to not only reap financial benefits but also support the global push towards sustainability.

Venture capital in the tech startup ecosystem is another avenue where investors can capitalise on emerging trends. Startups are often at the forefront of innovation, unencumbered by the bureaucratic inertia that larger corporations may face. Supporting early-stage tech startups can be high-risk, but the potential for high-reward is substantial. Investors need to conduct thorough due diligence, focusing on the feasibility of the business model, the market need, and the team's ability to execute.

The remote work revolution, accelerated by the COVID-19 pandemic, has spurred demand for technologies that enable virtual collaboration and productivity. Companies focusing on developing software for virtual meetings, project management, and cloud storage are gaining traction. Investing in these companies can be particularly attractive as remote work—and hybrid working models—are likely to persist long into the future.

In summary, the myriad of tech-enabled investment opportunities available today offer investors the chance to engage with and shape the future economy. The intersection of technology with different sectors not only promises high financial returns but also drives considerable social and environmental impact. By aligning investment strategies with these tech trends, investors can position themselves at the forefront of the next wave of economic growth.

Ultimately, the key to successful tech-enabled investments lies in understanding the broader context in which these technologies operate. This requires a forward-looking perspective, a willingness to embrace change, and a discerning eye to identify which technologies are poised to disrupt existing paradigms. With thoughtful and strategic investment, the possibilities are boundless.

Chapter 21:
Social and Ethical Investments

We've explored the facets of a youthful and sustainable economy, from tech-fuelled disruptions to new modes of transportation. Now, we must turn our attention to the moral and ethical dimensions that accompany modern investment practices. The modern investor is not just looking for financial returns but also seeks to generate a positive societal impact.

Social and ethical investments have grown from niche interests to mainstream considerations. Investors are asking challenging questions about where their money goes and the real-world impact it creates. Questions regarding environmental sustainability, social justice, and corporate governance are at the forefront of investment decisions. This interest mirrors a shift in consumer behaviour, reflecting a heightened sense of responsibility and awareness.

It's essential to distinguish between different forms of ethical investment: socially responsible investing (SRI), environmental, social, and governance (ESG) investing, and impact investing. While these terms are often used interchangeably, they serve distinct purposes and embody different strategies. SRI aims to avoid investments in companies that contradict ethical values, such as tobacco firms or weapons manufacturers. ESG investing evaluates an investment's implications across environmental, social, and governance parameters. In contrast, impact investing goes a step further, targeting investments that actively seek to create social or environmental good, often in measurable terms.

The rationale behind these investments is compelling. Ethical investments can lead to sustainable growth, risk mitigation, and, crucially, alignment with personal or institutional values. These investments provide an opportunity to endorse causes that matter to investors, while still achieving financial gains. Aligning one's portfolio with their principles is not just about feeling good—it's a strategic move that resonates with the demands of future generations.

Take climate change, for instance. Companies that invest in clean energy technologies or sustainable agricultural practices not only position themselves as leaders in innovation but also mitigate the long-term risks associated with environmental degradation. Climate-related risks are not speculative; they are already influencing market stability and asset values. Thus, an awareness of ESG criteria can serve as a hedge against future market volatility.

Yet, the path to integrating social and ethical frameworks into investment strategies is riddled with challenges. One significant hurdle is the absence of universal metrics for measuring social and ethical impact. While financial performance can be quantified with relative ease, the same cannot be said for societal impact. Investors must often rely on third-party ratings or proprietary analytics, which can sometimes offer inconsistent or conflicting information.

An additional barrier arises from the perceived trade-off between ethical considerations and financial performance. However, recent studies increasingly debunk this myth, suggesting that ESG-related investments perform on par with, if not better than, traditional investments over the long term. These findings have significantly altered the investment landscape, making it more appealing for those who want their money to work harder and smarter.

It's imperative to consider the evolving landscape of corporate governance. Today's investors are not passive stakeholders; they are active participants influencing corporate strategies. Shareholder activism has become a potent force in steering companies towards more sustainable practices. Investors wielding significant influence can advocate for changes in corporate policies, from carbon footprint reductions to diversity and inclusion initiatives.

Moreover, social and ethical investments aren't restricted to high-profile public corporations. Microfinance initiatives, community bonds, and social enterprises offer lucrative avenues for impactful investments. For instance, microfinance institutions provide financial services to underserved communities, fostering entrepreneurship and economic empowerment at the grassroots level.

Ethical investments also afford the means to tackle pressing social issues like inequality and access to education. Funds that focus on educational technologies or affordable housing can generate significant social dividends, transforming lives while offering investors a stake in high-growth sectors. The ripple effect of such investments extends beyond immediate beneficiaries, contributing to a more inclusive and equitable society.

Yet, the effectiveness of these investments requires ongoing scrutiny and adaptability. Ethical investment strategies must evolve to address new challenges and emerging trends. Investors must remain vigilant and informed, regularly reassessing their portfolios to ensure alignment with both their financial goals and ethical standards.

The rise of digital platforms has democratised access to social and ethical investments. Crowdfunding and peer-to-peer lending platforms offer opportunities for smaller investors to participate in impactful ventures. These platforms not only provide essential capital for innovative projects but also foster a community-driven approach to investment.

As impactful as these strategies can be, they're not without their ethical dilemmas. The ethical landscape is complex and multifaceted. For instance, an investment in renewable energy might inadvertently support brownfield developments, sparking debates on the true cost and value of such investments. These nuances require a conscientious approach, making it crucial for investors to conduct thorough due diligence.

The regulatory environment also plays a crucial role in shaping the landscape of social and ethical investments. Legislation such as the EU's Sustainable Finance Disclosure Regulation (SFDR) aims to bring transparency to sustainable investments, helping investors make more informed choices. As the regulatory framework continues to evolve, it will likely heighten scrutiny and encourage best practices across the industry.

In conclusion, social and ethical investments present a compelling case for the modern investor. They align financial returns with personal values, promote sustainable growth, and address some of the most pressing societal issues of our time. As we've seen, the journey is fraught with challenges, but the rewards extend far beyond financial gain. By incorporating ethical considerations into their investment strategies, investors can contribute to a more sustainable and equitable future, one investment at a time.

Chapter 22:
Leveraging Big Data to
Understand Youth Markets

In the rapidly evolving landscape of investment, understanding youth markets is not merely advantageous—it's essential. Big Data, a term that encapsulates vast quantities of unstructured and structured data, offers unparalleled insights into the preferences, behaviours, and trends of young consumers. By effectively leveraging this data, investors can gain a decisive edge in forecasting market trends and making well-informed decisions.

Youth markets are distinct in their evolving preferences and dynamic nature. Traditional methods of market analysis often fall short of capturing these quick shifts. Enter Big Data: it consolidates information from diverse sources like social media platforms, online transactions, mobile apps, and more. This data can reveal trends almost in real-time, offering investors actionable insights into the younger demographic's evolving tastes and preferences.

The first step in leveraging Big Data is to identify the key sources of data collection. Social media platforms such as Instagram, Twitter, and TikTok are treasure troves of information. Young consumers express their desires, protest against brands, and rally behind causes on these platforms. By analysing posts, hashtags, likes, shares, and comments, investors can gauge public sentiment and predict upcoming trends.

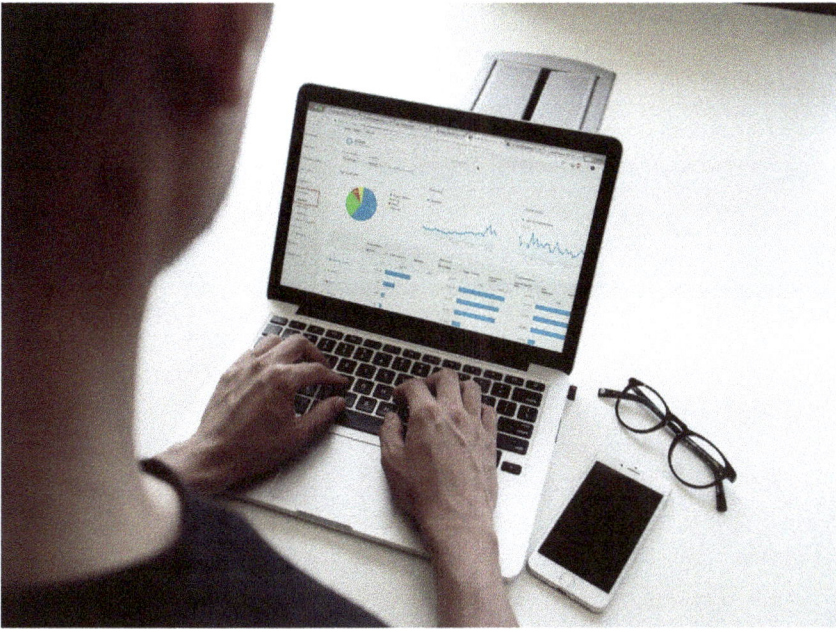

Structured data, such as transaction histories, provides another layer of narrative. Analysing purchase patterns and preferences can reveal what products are gaining traction among youths. One notable example is the rise in demand for sustainable products. Transaction data has shown an increase in purchases of eco-friendly and ethically sourced items, underscoring the younger generation's commitment to sustainability.

Big Data analytics also enables segmentation of the youth market into various personas. By examining factors such as geographical location, socioeconomic status, and education level, investors can create more nuanced profiles of young consumers. This segmentation allows for targeted marketing and investment strategies, significantly increasing the probability of success.

Machine learning algorithms and artificial intelligence (AI) further amplify the power of Big Data. These technologies can identify patterns that may not be immediately apparent to human analysts. For instance, AI can predict fashion trends based on a combination of social media activity and historical sales data. This predictive capability is invaluable for investors aiming to stay ahead of the curve.

However, leveraging Big Data is not without its challenges. Data privacy is a major concern. With stringent regulations such as the General Data Protection Regulation (GDPR) in the EU and the California Consumer Privacy Act (CCPA) in the USA, navigating the legal landscape becomes crucial. Investors must ensure that their data collection and analysis methods are compliant with these regulations to avoid legal repercussions.

Another challenge is the integration of disparate data sources. Big Data is often siloed, originating from various systems that don't naturally communicate with one another. Integrating these data streams requires sophisticated data management systems and skilled personnel to derive actionable insights effectively. Nonetheless, the benefits far outweigh these challenges.

Real-time data analytics offers one of the most compelling advantages of leveraging Big Data. The ability to monitor trends as they emerge ensures that investors can make timely decisions. For example, if a new app becomes wildly popular among teenagers overnight, investors who are monitoring social media can quickly capitalise on this trend. Rapid response to market shifts is an invaluable asset in today's fast-paced economy.

In addition to understanding consumer preferences, Big Data can also offer insights into youth employment trends. By analysing job search patterns, educational enrolment data, and career-related social media posts, investors can identify which industries are becoming more popular among young professionals. This information is crucial for directing investments towards sectors likely to see growth due to an influx of young talent.

The utility of Big Data extends beyond consumer behaviour and employment trends; it also encompasses societal values and ethical considerations. Young consumers often prioritise companies that align with their values. By analysing social media discussions and online activism, investors can understand the ethical and social priorities of the younger demographic. This enables the creation of portfolios that not only promise profitability but also resonate with ethical standards.

Collaborations between data scientists and industry experts can further refine the insights gained from Big Data. While data scientists excel at extracting patterns and correlations, industry experts provide context, ensuring the data translates into practical investment strategies. This interdisciplinary approach maximises the utility of Big Data, offering a comprehensive understanding of youth markets.

Predictive analytics, a key facet of Big Data, offers another layer of foresight. By employing statistical algorithms, investors can forecast future trends based on historical data. This predictive power is crucial for long-term investments, enabling stakeholders to make preemptive moves rather than reactive adjustments. For instance, if predictive models indicate a growing preference for renewable energy among young consumers, investors can allocate resources accordingly, ensuring sustained growth.

Furthermore, Big Data facilitates customisation at scale. Personalised marketing campaigns, informed by detailed consumer profiles, can significantly enhance engagement rates. When young consumers feel that products or services are tailored to their unique preferences, their likelihood of purchase increases. This personalisation is achievable through the detailed insights provided by Big Data, making it a formidable tool for maximizing returns on investment.

In terms of execution, leveraging Big Data requires a robust IT infrastructure. Cloud computing solutions offer scalable storage and processing power necessary for analysing large datasets. Partnering with tech firms that specialise in Big Data analytics can further streamline this process, enabling investors to focus on strategic decision-making rather than the technical intricacies of data management.

As we look to the future, it's clear that the integration of Big Data in understanding youth markets will become even more sophisticated. Emerging technologies such as the Internet of Things (IoT) and blockchain are poised to provide even richer, more secure datasets. These advancements will further empower investors to make informed decisions, ensuring their portfolios are aligned with the latest trends and ethical considerations.

In conclusion, the strategic use of Big Data offers a multifaceted approach to understanding youth markets. From predicting consumer preferences to identifying employment trends and aligning with societal values, Big Data provides a comprehensive toolkit for investors. The ability to rapidly adapt to market shifts, coupled with predictive capabilities and personalised strategies, positions investors to leverage the youthful and sustainable economy of tomorrow effectively.

The journey of adapting to and utilising Big Data is ongoing, but the rewards are substantial. By embracing this powerful tool, investors not only gain a competitive edge but also contribute to shaping a market that reflects the values and aspirations of the younger generation. This alignment ensures a sustainable and profitable future, resonating deeply with the ethos of the youth-driven market.

Chapter 23:
The Role of Governments and NGOs

The landscape of investment is increasingly shaped by the interactions between governments, non-governmental organisations (NGOs), and the private sector. In the youthful and sustainable economy of tomorrow, understanding these dynamics is critical for investors. Governments and NGOs influence market conditions, regulatory frameworks, and societal trends, thereby indirectly steering the trajectory of potential returns on investments.

Governments play a pivotal role by setting policies that either encourage or hinder investment opportunities. Policy frameworks around renewable energy, digital infrastructure, education, and healthcare have a substantial impact on profitability and long-term viability. For instance, government subsidies in renewable energy not only promote environmental sustainability but also create lucrative opportunities for investors willing to dive into green technologies.

Take Germany's Energiewende (Energy Transition) initiative as an example. By heavily subsidising renewable energy projects, the German government has spurred innovation and investment in wind and solar technologies. Investors who tapped into this market early reaped significant rewards, demonstrating the importance of aligning investment strategies with governmental policies.

However, navigating governmental influences involves more than just identifying favourable policies. Investors need to be aware of potential regulatory risks. Changes in leadership, political instability, or shifts in public opinion can lead to sudden policy reversals, impacting the investment landscape. A diversified portfolio, with a keen understanding of regional policy environments, can mitigate such risks.

Non-governmental organisations (NGOs), on the other hand, bring a different kind of influence. NGOs often function as the societal conscience, focusing on issues that governments may overlook or underprioritise. They advocate for sustainable practices, social equity, and ethical governance—all factors increasingly important to the young, conscientious investor.

Consider how NGOs have shaped corporate behaviours through advocacy and direct action. Organisations like Greenpeace and the World Wildlife Fund have successfully pressured industries to adopt more sustainable practices. These shifts, driven by NGO influence, create new realms for investment that align with both ethical standards and profitability. When corporations adapt to meet the demands of conscientious consumers, they often open up new market segments ripe for investment.

It's imperative to examine how NGOs indirectly affect market environments. Through awareness campaigns and direct intervention, NGOs can alter consumer preferences and expectations. For example, the rising popularity of ethical consumption can be attributed to persistent NGO campaigns highlighting issues like fair trade and human rights. Investors who are attuned to these shifts can strategically align their portfolios to match evolving consumer values.

Furthermore, the collaboration between governments and NGOs frequently leads to innovative public-private partnerships. These collaborations can result in hybrid investment models that leverage the strengths of each sector. Governments provide regulatory support and initial funding, while NGOs bring expertise and credibility. The private sector, powered by investors, delivers scalability and innovation.

One prominent example is the Global Alliance for Vaccines and Immunisation (GAVI). This partnership between governments, NGOs, and the private sector has not only improved global health outcomes but also created a thriving market for vaccine-related investments. Such synergies offer pathways to investment opportunities that not only promise returns but also contribute to broader societal good.

In focusing on long-term sustainability, both governments and NGOs play integral roles in setting agendas and benchmarks. Investors must track significant policy documents, international accords, and NGO reports to stay ahead of the curve. Documents like the Paris Agreement and the United Nations Sustainable Development Goals (SDGs) serve as roadmaps for future investment landscapes.

It's clear that the intersection of governmental policy and NGO advocacy shapes the contours of sustainable investments. But it also highlights a vital consideration: the alignment of investment strategies with global sustainability goals isn't merely ethical but profitable. Investors who heed these trends can uncover opportunities that promise growth, stability, and ethical alignment.

Therefore, scrutinising the policy arena and NGO activities offers not just a defensive strategy against market volatility but also a proactive approach to capturing emerging sectors and trends. In doing so, investors can ensure that their portfolios reflect the multifaceted dimensions of a youthful and sustainable economy, setting the stage for robust and responsible financial growth.

Investors should also consider the unique roles that regional governments and NGOs play. Emerging markets, often characterised by younger demographics, provide diverse opportunities and challenges. Governments in these regions may offer incentives to attract foreign investment, while local NGOs can offer on-the-ground insights and facilitate entry into these markets. Recognising and adapting to the local context is crucial for maximising returns in these environments.

One cannot overlook the importance of geopolitical stability in investment decisions. Stable governments with transparent regulatory frameworks offer a predictable investment climate. Conversely, regions plagued by conflict or corruption present significant risks. NGOs, with their extensive networks and local knowledge, can serve as valuable partners in assessing and navigating these risks.

Finally, as digital transformation accelerates, both governments and NGOs are leveraging technology to enhance transparency and accountability. Blockchain technology, for example, is being explored to track environmental impacts and ensure ethical supply chains. These innovations not only build investor confidence but also open up new areas for investment in tech-driven solutions. Being at the forefront of such technological advancements can offer investors a competitive edge in an increasingly digital world.

In conclusion, the interplay between governments, NGOs, and the private sector is fundamental to shaping a youthful and sustainable economy. By understanding the roles and influences of these entities, investors can better navigate the complexities of the modern investment landscape, aligning their strategies with broader societal goals and emerging market trends. Investing with an eye on these dynamics ensures not only financial returns but also contributes to the development of a more equitable and sustainable future.

Chapter 24:
Preparing for Demographic Shifts

In navigating the complexities of future investment landscapes, it's vital to consider demographic shifts as dynamic forces shaping economies. Investors who align their strategies with demographic realities will find themselves better positioned to capitalise on emerging opportunities. Anticipating changes in population structures requires a comprehensive understanding of the underlying trends and their implications on various sectors.

The globe is witnessing a significant demographic transition, driven by declining fertility rates and increasing life expectancy. The resultant ageing population poses challenges and opportunities for investors. While sectors like healthcare and retirement planning will undoubtedly benefit, other areas may face reduced demand. An older population changes consumption patterns, necessitating a shift in how portfolios are structured.

A major point of consideration is the burgeoning influence of younger demographics in certain regions. Africa and parts of Asia, for example, boast youthful populations that promise economic vibrancy. These regions provide fertile ground for investments in education, technology, and consumer goods tailored to a younger audience. Investors must, therefore, balance opportunities arising from both ageing and youthful populations.

Urbanisation is another trend accompanying demographic shifts. As more people migrate to cities, the strain on urban infrastructure becomes apparent, yet so do investment opportunities. Real estate in urban centres will likely see increased demand, but there's also a growing need for innovative solutions in transport, housing, and public utilities. Poulating urban centres will be at the heart of economic activities, driving growth in multiple sectors.

Understanding Demographic Shifts and Their Impact

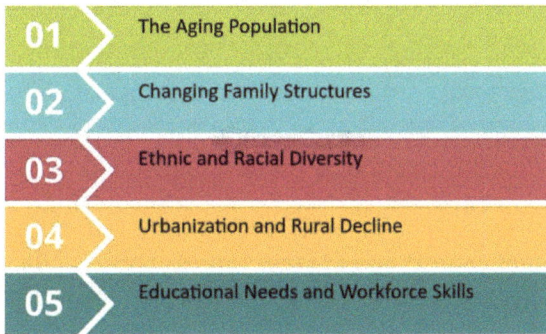

01	The Aging Population
02	Changing Family Structures
03	Ethnic and Racial Diversity
04	Urbanization and Rural Decline
05	Educational Needs and Workforce Skills

Alongside urbanisation, the changing workforce demographics cannot be ignored. With more women entering the workforce and increased demand for flexible working conditions, businesses must adapt, and investors should look favourably upon those that do. Companies with inclusive policies and those investing in remote work technologies are poised to thrive. Small yet pivotal shifts in workforce demographics can reshape the competitive landscape.

It's also crucial to consider the role of migration in demographic changes. Migration patterns, whether driven by economic opportunities or political strife, reshape the social and economic fabric of host countries. Countries that attract skilled migrants benefit from an influx of talent and innovation, essential for sectors like technology and engineering. Keen investors must monitor migration trends, as these influxes often signal emerging markets and sectors poised for growth.

Next, we turn to the digital economy, which stands at the intersection of multiple demographic trends. The younger, tech-savvy generation drives the rapid adoption of digital technologies, while older generations increasingly see the benefits of digital inclusion. The convergence of these trends means that investments in digital infrastructure and cybersecurity are no longer optional—they're imperative. Technology unites various demographic segments, creating a rich mosaic of opportunities for astute investors.

However, an ageing population presents unique challenges. Healthcare becomes a critical area for investment. The need for a robust healthcare infrastructure, including hospitals, clinics, and telemedicine, grows exponentially. Investors must also consider ancillary services, such as medical devices and pharmaceuticals, which will see sustained demand. Aligning investment portfolios to cater to these needs will ensure resilience against demographic shifts.

Moreover, the financial products designed for retirement planning and elder care insurance are set to expand. The demand for long-term care facilities and age-friendly housing will rise sharply. Understanding these niche markets allows investors to diversify portfolios, ensuring that the demographic transition is not only accounted for but optimally leveraged.

Another salient point is educational investments tailored to younger demographics in emerging markets. As youthful populations in regions like Sub-Saharan Africa and South Asia strive for better futures, investments in educational technologies and institutions provide substantial returns. Educated young populations are catalysts for economic growth, driving innovation and consumption. By prioritising education, investors lay the groundwork for long-term socio-economic stability and progress.

Environmental consciousness among younger generations also warrants attention. There's a dramatic shift towards sustainability and ethical consumption. That means investments in green technologies, renewable energy, and sustainably produced goods are not just trendy—they're future-proof. The commitment to sustainability reflects broader demographic values that will only gain prominence as these younger cohorts age.

Moreover, the intersection of demographic shifts and policy changes plays a pivotal role. Governments worldwide are enacting policies to address the needs of ageing populations while stimulating youth employment. Policies promoting workforce retraining, age-friendly workplaces, and youth entrepreneurship support these demographic realities. Savvy investors understand that policy and regulation are not hurdles but signals indicating where resources may best be allocated. Attention to policy can thus translate into strategic, well-timed investments.

Understanding regional variations in demographic trends offers another layer of precision in investment strategy. Europe and Japan, for instance, face mature economies with slower population growth and significant ageing issues. Contrast this with Latin America and Southeast Asia, where populations remain relatively young and economically active. Customising investment approaches to reflect these regional differences allows for a nuanced and impactful investment strategy.

In recognising these shifts, scenario planning becomes an essential tool for investors. By envisaging different future scenarios driven by demographic changes, investors can model potential outcomes and devise versatile strategies. Whether considering high-growth youth markets or mature economies coping with ageing populations, scenario planning offers a robust framework for decision-making.

Interestingly, the convergence of several small demographic trends often spurs significant market transformations. Retail investors need to think about these converging trends carefully. The rise of the gig economy, increased life expectancies, urbanisation, and migration collectively contribute to a rapidly evolving economic landscape. Investors can seize compelling opportunities by weaving together insights from these distinct yet interconnected shifts.

The prudent investor must continuously refine their understanding of demographic data and trends. Regularly revisiting census data, migration reports, and workforce studies ensures that one's investment strategy remains aligned with ever-changing realities. This dynamic approach to investment—a blend of data, foresight, and agility—ensures long-term success in a shifting demographic landscape.

In summary, preparing for demographic shifts is not merely about recognising population changes but understanding their broader economic implications. Investors who adeptly navigate these shifts, appreciate regional nuances, and align their strategies with demographic trends will find themselves not only resilient but also prosperous in the coming decades. By investing in key areas such as healthcare, education, technology, and sustainable practices, they will be ready to harness the potential of a youthful and sustainable global economy.

Chapter 25:
Future Scenarios and
Investment Strategies

A s we approach the future's myriad potentialities, investors must keenly focus on emerging scenarios that could shape markets. Today's informed decisions hinge on a subtle understanding of the interplay between youthful consumer behaviour and broader economic trends. This chapter explores various future scenarios and distills strategic investment approaches tailored to these evolving landscapes.

Predictive Analysis of Emerging Markets

To navigate future uncertainties, predictive analysis anchored in historical data and current innovations proves indispensable. The youth's predilection for technology and sustainability suggests a gravitation towards markets that exemplify these values. Hence, sectors such as renewable energy, biotechnology, and digital assets are gaining traction. Furthermore, we've witnessed remarkable shifts in consumer preferences, necessitating a forward-looking investment ethos.

Consider renewable energy. Once a niche investment, it's now a cornerstone in diversified portfolios. Escalating environmental concerns and improving technologies present a compelling narrative. As the global pivot towards net-zero emissions accelerates, supporting ventures in green energy becomes not merely a moral choice but a financially astute one. Imagine a world where clean energy isn't an alternative but the standard. Investments today could catalyse such a paradigm shift tomorrow.

The Transformational Power of Technology

Technological advancements are unmasking new opportunities and risks. Artificial intelligence, blockchain, and the Internet of Things are no longer futuristic concepts but viable sectors. Investing in companies that pioneer in these domains offers prospects of exponential growth. Yet, diversification within these fields is crucial, given their profound interdependencies and rapidly evolving nature.

Consider artificial intelligence. From healthcare to financial services, AI is revolutionising entire industries, making processes more efficient and unlocking new capabilities. Investments in AI-oriented startups or ETFs could yield considerable returns. However, investors should remain cognisant of regulatory landscapes, as policy changes could either bolster or stymie growth in these areas.

Sustainable Consumerism as a Market Driver

Sustainable consumerism isn't just a buzzword; it's crystallising into a dominant market driver. The younger generation's insistence on ethical and eco-friendly products signals robust future markets for firms aligning with these values. Therefore, investments in companies prioritising sustainability—whether through eco-friendly products, transparent supply chains, or commitments to reducing carbon footprints—are likely to flourish.

Fashion and apparel industries are poignant examples. Fast fashion is facing backlash as consumers become more environmentally conscious. Brands prioritising sustainability are claiming larger market shares. This trend suggests opportunities not only in sustainable retail but also in the broader ecosystem, including technology that tracks and mitigates environmental impact.

Global Healthcare Evolutions

Healthcare continues to be an enduring sector, influenced significantly by technology and demographic shifts. Innovations in telemedicine, personalised treatment plans, and biotechnology are transforming patient care. Investments in these avenues promise resilience against economic fluctuations and align with long-term demographic trends, such as ageing populations and rising chronic diseases.

Biotechnology companies, in particular, have shown remarkable potential. Advances in gene therapy, regenerative medicine, and precision medicine underscore the sector's promise. Investors should watch emerging players and established firms alike, as strategic partnerships and groundbreaking innovations frequently shape this space.

Digitalisation and the Fintech Frontier

Fintech has emerged as a potent force, democratising access to financial services and innovating beyond traditional banking. With digital wallets, cryptocurrencies, and decentralised finance (DeFi) platforms revolutionising monetary systems, investors must heed these changes.

The traditional banking sector is not obsolete but increasingly finds itself competing against agile fintech firms offering more personalised and efficient services. Investments in fintech-specific funds or directly in leading companies can provide exposure to this dynamic landscape. However, awareness of regulatory mechanisms, especially with cryptocurrencies, remains crucial.

Unpredictable yet Fragile Geopolitical Landscapes

Geopolitical shifts are unpredictable yet crucial in shaping investment strategies. Trade policies, international alliances, and regulatory landscapes form a complex backdrop that can either enable or constrain economic opportunities. Thus, geopolitical analysis must complement market research.

For instance, the interplay of US-China relations can substantially influence technology and trade sectors. Diversifying investments geographically and across multiple industries can mitigate risks associated with such geopolitical instabilities, balancing your portfolio against sudden shifts in international relations.

Resilience through Diversification

Diversification remains a timeless strategy amid evolving markets. It's not just about scattering investments across various sectors but understanding the synergies and divergences amongst chosen assets. A balanced portfolio might include a mix of high-risk, high-reward stocks, stable blue-chip companies, and fixed-income securities. This balance can shield against volatilities while seizing growth opportunities.

Emerging markets, particularly in Asia and Africa, offer lucrative avenues. Rapid urbanisation and digital adoption in these regions suggest nascent markets ready to be tapped. Nevertheless, investors should tread cautiously, weighing stability against potential gains.

Ethical and Impact Investing

Youthful investors are increasingly prioritising ethical considerations in their investment decisions. Impact investing, where the focus is not just on financial returns but also social and environmental impacts, is accumulating interest. Funds explicitly designed to support social enterprises, renewable energy projects, and community development initiatives are exemplary of this trend.

Investors now have opportunities to align their portfolios with their value systems. Such alignment doesn't merely serve ethical satisfaction but often correlates with improved financial performance, as these ventures typically attract loyal customer bases and favourable regulatory conditions.

Building Knowledge Infrastructure

Ongoing education is paramount. The fast-paced nature of technological innovation, market dynamics, and global policies necessitates a continuous learning approach. Webinars, industry reports, and networking within investor communities can provide insights that refine investment strategies.

Moreover, building a knowledge infrastructure organically evolves into an appreciation for nuanced market movements, allowing investors to anticipate shifts before they become apparent to the broader market. This anticipatory acumen represent a distinct competitive advantage.

In sum, the road ahead demands agility, informed risk-taking, and a profound understanding of emerging trends. The investors who successfully navigate future scenarios will be those who intuitively blend conventional wisdom with contemporary insights.

As we transition towards a future pulsating with potential and complex challenges, aligning investment strategies with the evolving ethos of a youthful and sustainable economy will not only promise lucrative returns but also foster lasting positive impact. The future is not merely to be anticipated but actively shaped through conscious, informed decisions.

The strategies discussed aren't exhaustive but serve as guiding principles. Each investment decision should be underpinned by thorough research and nuanced understanding. The willingness to adapt and evolve remains the most valuable asset in an investor's toolkit in this dynamic, ever-changing landscape.

Conclusion

As we look ahead, it's clear that the youthful and sustainable economy isn't just a distant ideal but an imminent reality. Investors who are attuned to these unfolding dynamics stand to benefit considerably. Throughout this book, we've explored the myriad of factors shaping tomorrow's economic landscape—from the unique traits of digital natives to shifts in global connectivity and sustainability. In closing, we must synthesise these insights to carve out effective, forward-thinking investment strategies.

The youthful market is not merely a demographic segment; it's a harbinger of broader societal shifts. Each chapter has shown the profound impact young consumers are having across industries, from real estate to transportation. This generation prioritises experiences over ownership, values sustainability, and is embedded within a digital ecosystem. The wise investor recognises that these traits aren't fleeting trends but foundational to future market behaviour.

Indeed, the sustainability mindset can no longer be considered optional. It's essential. Companies and sectors that embrace environmentally friendly practices and policies not only meet the ethical standards of young consumers but also mitigate long-term risks. The push towards sustainability is backed by both consumer demand and regulatory landscapes. Therefore, aligning investment strategies with sustainable practices isn't a nicety—it's a necessity for ensuring robust, future-proofed portfolios.

Moreover, the importance of bridging the 'aspirations gap' cannot be overstated. Young consumers have high expectations and distinct needs. Investments that succeed will be those tuned to these aspirations, resonating authentically and meaningfully with the youth. This involves not only creating products and services that appeal but also communicating in ways that engage and inspire. Ignoring this emotional and psychological dimension may be a perilous oversight for any investor.

Disruptors shouldn't be viewed as threats but as opportunities. Companies like Octopus Energy exemplify how innovation can lead to more efficient, consumer-friendly solutions. The disruptors of today are likely to shape the standard practices of tomorrow. Hence, identifying and supporting these entities early can provide substantial returns while contributing to broader societal advancements.

The real estate sector, for instance, is undergoing transformative shifts driven by youthful preferences. Micro-living spaces, co-housing, and sustainable constructions are becoming the new norms. Investors should pivot towards these emerging trends to maximise their returns while promoting sustainable urban ecosystems. Similarly, the transportation realm is rapidly evolving, influenced by the need for greener, more efficient mobility solutions. Investing in electric vehicles, shared mobility services, and related infrastructures holds promise for both financial gains and environmental benefits.

In terms of food, the future belongs to innovative solutions addressing sustainability. From plant-based diets to vertical farming, new paradigms in food production and consumption are being established. This sector will likely continue to expand, presenting numerous opportunities for investment.

On the broader economic canvas, adapting to changes in employment trends is crucial. Youth employment is becoming increasingly digital and entrepreneurial. A focus on start-ups and tech-enabled solutions offers a fertile ground for innovative investment. Ventures that support entrepreneurial efforts and digital empowerment will likely stand out in tomorrow's economy.

Furthermore, the landscape of financial products is evolving. New financial instruments tailored to younger generations' needs are emerging. These include fintech solutions, peer-to-peer lending platforms, and more. Investors who can navigate and leverage these innovations will find themselves well-positioned in the market.

In the intertwining realms of education and sustainability, forward-thinking investments will enable economic and ecological benefits. The rising demand for sustainable educational frameworks indicates that support for such initiatives could offer significant returns, both financially and societally.

Understanding and leveraging big data is crucial. Big data analytics can provide unprecedented insights into youthful preferences and behaviours, guiding more informed investment decisions. Harnessing this data will be instrumental in developing targeted, effective strategies that resonate with young consumers.

Finally, the role of government and NGOs is instrumental in shaping the economic landscape. Policies and initiatives that support sustainable and innovative practices provide a robust framework for investments to thrive. Therefore, a keen understanding of policy influence is necessary for aligning investments with broader economic objectives.

To conclude, preparing for demographic shifts and anticipating future scenarios are no longer optional for prudent investing—they are imperative. Financial markets are on the cusp of transformation driven by youthful energy and sustainable imperatives. This book intends to serve as a comprehensive guide, equipping investors with the knowledge and insight to make informed, future-proof decisions.

The youthful economy, intertwined with sustainability principles, presents both challenges and opportunities. By staying adaptable, forward-thinking, and attuned to youthful and environmental demands, investors can not only achieve significant financial returns but also contribute to a prosperous, sustainable future.

In essence, investing in tomorrow's world is about more than profit—it's about stewardship, vision, and a commitment to a better, more sustainable world. The decisions we make today will shape the economy of tomorrow. Let's make them count.

Appendix A:
Appendix

This appendix serves as a supplementary resource for investors aiming to navigate the youthful and sustainable economy of tomorrow. The objective is to provide actionable insights and practical advice relevant to each chapter discussed within the book.

Glossary of Terms

The glossary serves as a quick reference guide for key terms and concepts used throughout the book:

- **Digital Natives:** Individuals born or brought up during the age of digital technology and so are familiar with computers and the internet from an early age.

- **Sustainability:** Meeting our own needs without compromising the ability of future generations to meet their own needs.

- **Disruptors:** Companies or technologies that drastically alter or replace existing markets and value networks.

- **Experience Economy:** An economy in which the emphasis is on the provision of experiences rather than goods and services.

Additional Resources

For those seeking deeper knowledge in specific areas discussed in the book, the following resources are recommended:

1. **Books:**

   o Investing in the Age of Millennials by Barbara Atkins

   o The Circular Economy Handbook by Walter Stahel

   o The Sharing Economy by Arun Sundararajan

2. **Articles:**

   o "The Rise of Digital Natives" in The Economist

   o "Sustainability and You" by Harvard Business Review

   o "Disruptors of Tomorrow" in Financial Times

   o Gomes, Sofia, et al. "Willingness to Pay More for Green Products: A Critical Challenge for Gen Z." *Journal of Cleaner Production*, vol. 390, Mar. 2023, pp. 136092–136092, doi:10.1016/j.jclepro.2023.136092.

   o Rimanoczy, Isabel, and Beate Klingenberg. "The Sustainability Mindset Indicator: A Personal Development Tool." *Journal of Management for Global Sustainability*, vol. 9, no. 1, July 2021, pp. 43–79, doi:10.13185/jm2021.09103.

   o Tran, Trung, et al. "How Digital Natives Learn and Thrive in the Digital Age: Evidence from an Emerging Economy." *Sustainability*, vol. 12, no. 9, May 2020, pp. 3819–3819, doi:10.3390/su12093819.

   o Sher, Ali, et al. "Fostering Sustainable Ventures: Drivers of Sustainable Start-up Intentions among Aspiring Entrepreneurs in Pakistan." *Journal of Cleaner Production*, vol. 262, July 2020, pp. 121269–121269, doi:10.1016/j.jclepro.2020.121269.

3. **Websites and Blogs:**

- o <u>World Economic Forum</u>
- o <u>GreenBiz</u>
- o <u>TechCrunch</u>

Research Methodologies

A variety of research methods were utilised to compile the insights provided in this book, ensuring credibility and relevance. Methods include:

- **Quantitative Analysis:** Extensive use of data analytics and statistical tools to identify trends and patterns.

- **Qualitative Research:** Conducting interviews and focus groups with industry experts, as well as case studies from leading companies.

- **Literature Review:** Thorough review of existing literature and recent publications to provide a broad context.

Acknowledgements

We extend our gratitude to the many contributors and experts whose insights and feedback have been invaluable in making this book a definitive guide for investors. Special thanks go to:

- The editorial team for their relentless effort.

- The industry experts who shared their invaluable knowledge.

- The research assistants for their meticulous data gathering.

Contact Information

For any queries, suggestions, or further discussions, please reach out to us at:

Email: <u>hello@helix.earth</u>

Phone: +44-73882 55034

Thank you for embarking on this journey towards understanding and investing in a youthful and sustainable future.

www.ingramcontent.com/pod-product-compliance
Lightning Source LLC
Chambersburg PA
CBHW040927210326
41597CB00030B/5211